THE THEOLOGY
OF
MARTIN LUTHER

Five Contemporary Canadian Interpretations

edited by

Egil Grislis

1985

Canadian Cataloguing in Publication Data

Main entry under title:

The Theology of Martin Luther

Essays originally presented at the Luther
    Symposium, held in Waterloo, Ont., Oct. 31-
    Nov. 1, 1983.
ISBN 0-919599-24-9

1. Luther, Martin, 1483-1546-Theology-
Addresses, essays, lectures. I. Grislis, Egil,
1928-   II. Luther Symposium (1983 : Waterloo,
Ont.)
BR333.2.T53 1985   230'.41'0924   C85-091117-6

To *William E. Hordern*
in esteem and friendship.

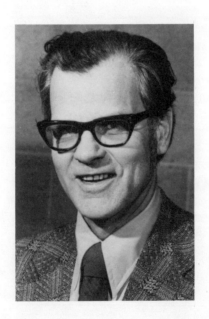

INTRODUCTION

Though born five centuries ago, Martin Luther has made an impact which is still being felt in our own day. Authentic faith is indeed essentially indestructible. To reflect on Luther's faith the Division of Theology of the Lutheran Council in Canada sponsored a Luther Symposium from October 31 to November 1, 1983, in Waterloo, Ontario. Interpreted in the perspective of the United Church of Canada, an ecumenical Roman Catholic viewpoint, as well as the Mennonite and Lutheran traditions, Luther emerged in an exciting, although not uniform way.

A man of deep, biblical faith and real courage, Luther continues to challenge in the study of the Holy Bible, often serves as a catalyst in the formation of faith, and steadfastly warns against any cheap compromise. Modern Luther scholarship—for some decades now no longer limited to "Lutherans only"—has done much to clarify Luther's creative insights as well as to note some of his potential weaknesses. While admittedly limited in scope, the present volume of essays seeks to provide a guide to the contemporary understanding of Luther in Canada.

The Luther Symposium, at which these essays were originally delivered, was organized by the Reverend Norman J. Threinen, Th.D., then Executive Secretary of the Division of Theology of the Lutheran Council in Canada, and now Professor at Concordia Lutheran Seminary in Edmonton, Alberta. The Symposium was enabled through a grant from the Lutheran Life Insurance Society of Canada. The essays were chosen for publication by the Division of Theology of the Lutheran Council in Canada. The generous financial support for the printing of this volume has been supplied by the Lutheran Council in Canada and by a fraternal grant from the members of the Lutheran Life Insurance Society of Canada.

Gratitude is also expressed to T. and T. Clark, Ltd., Edinburgh, for the permission to include the essay by Dr. Harry McSorley, and to Ms. Esther Koslowsky for her expert typing of the manuscript.

This volume is dedicated in gratitude to the Reverend Dr. William E. Hordern, for the past two decades President of the Lutheran Theological Seminary at Saskatoon, Saskatchewan, and a renowned Canadian Luther scholar.

Egil Grislis

CONTRIBUTORS:

DR. H. GORDON HARLAND is the Head of the Department of Religion at the University of Manitoba. A native of Manitoba, he has studied and taught at several universities in Canada and the United States. He has authored *The Thought of Reinhold Niebuhr* and numerous articles on religion in North America.

DR. HARRY McSORLEY is Professor in the Religious Studies Department of the University of Toronto and in the Faculty of Theology of St. Michael's College in the Toronto School of Theology. He has studied at both Catholic and Protestant theological faculties in Germany. He has been a member of the U.S.A. National Consultation between Lutherans and Roman Catholics and now serves on the Anglican-Roman Catholic Consultation in Canada. He is the author of *Luther: Right or Wrong?*, a contributor to *The Role of the Augsburg Confession: Catholic and Lutheran Views* and numerous other books and articles.

DR. HARRY LOEWEN is Professor of German and Mennonite Studies at the University of Winnipeg. A native of the Ukraine, he attended public schools in the Soviet Union and Germany and studied at several universities in Manitoba and Ontario. Among his many publications are books on *Luther and the Radicals, Goethe's Response to Protestantism, Mennonite Images,* and articles on Luther, the Anabaptists, and German literature.

DR. LOWELL C. GREEN, until recently Professor of Historical and Systematic Theology at Concordia Lutheran Theological Seminary in St. Catharines, is presently Pastor of Gethsemane Lutheran Church, Buffalo, New York. A native of the United States, he also studied in Germany. His doctoral dissertation at the University of Erlangen compared Melanchthon and Luther on the doctrine of Justification. He has taught at several seminaries and universities in the United States, is also an accomplished church musician, and has authored numerous books and articles in theology, worship and education.

DR. EGIL GRISLIS is Professor of Religion at the University of Manitoba. A native of Latvia, he has also studied in Germany and the United States. His dissertation at Yale was entitled "Luther's Understanding of the Wrath of God." In addition to the University of Manitoba, he has taught at several universities in the United States. He has edited and written on a broad range of topics, including studies on Luther, Calvin, Menno Simons and Richard Hooker.

TABLE OF CONTENTS

I THE CONTEMPORARY RELEVANCE OF MARTIN LUTHER

by
H. Gordon Harland

In a recent article in *The New York Times Magazine*, Jaroslav Pelikan introduced his discussion of Martin Luther with a remarkable statement. Said Pelikan: "The most exciting and most controversial figure in Christian thought today is probably a man who was born 500 years ago."[1] That judgement can certainly be debated but the fact that it can be seriously presented and found at all plausible is an astonishing fact. And it clearly indicates what it is we are doing when we study Luther's work and legacy and when we celebrate the 500th anniversary of his birth.

We are not engaged in some ritual of nostalgia, some exercise of filial piety limited to a narrow denominational concern. Nor are we pursuing the kind of academic inquiry that is restricted to those of highly specialized or esoteric interests. No. To engage the thought of Luther and the revolution he set loose is to find ourselves wrestling with the message of the Gospel, the state of contemporary society, the condition of the separate churches, their relation to the whole Christian heritage, and the role they are playing or failing to play in the culture of our day. Because of this, Luther is indeed a figure of great contemporary as well as historical importance.

The reason why Luther possesses this remarkable capacity is, of course, a question of prime importance, and there is no simple answer to it. Several years ago, Gordon Rupp, the distinguished Luther scholar—and English Methodist—made a remark that provides us with a pretty good handle in our attempt to come to grips with that question. Alluding to the tremendous forces for change that were at work in the sixteenth century, Rupp urged that "We must take into full account the vast political, economic and social pressures which were transforming Luther's world and with which a sick and enfeebled Church was quite incapable of coping." Then Rupp went on to say: "What Luther did was to make sure that if there should be conflict in Christendom it should be the right fight in the right place. But for him the Reformation movement must have centred in...secondary issues...."[2] That is a momentous statement. For just consider for a moment how easy it would have been for the whole movement to have been overwhelmed by the energies of nationalism fed by a thousand grievances; or how natural it would have been for all reforming energies to have been absorbed in the piecemeal correction of any number of ecclesiastical abuses and structural weaknesses. Or indeed how readily the whole Reformation could have been engulfed in a tide of human greed and passion. Just to mention these forces and possibilities is to glimpse something of Luther's achievement.

The Reformation, like all great historical movements, gathered all sorts of concerns and issues to itself. If, despite the great mixture of causes and motives that inevitably entered into the movement, Luther saw to it, as Rupp contended, that such an epochal event involved the right fight and if he did make sure that his message did not get centred in and swallowed up by secondary issues, then we have some insight into his historical greatness and contemporary relevance. The English historian, G.R. Elton, would seem to concur with this judgement. "The Reformation," remarks Elton, "was a revolution. So much is plain, but it is easy to mistake the nature of that revolution." And he goes on to note how often the Reformation is still understood as primarily an attack on the abuses in the Church—"immoral popes, corrupt clergy, idle monks, a weak and vacillating Christianity"—in short, as an attack on the "outward behaviour" of the Church of the day. To be sure, moral indignation certainly played an important role, but Elton rightly insists that this concentration on "abuses" missed the major point and the real revolution. As he puts it: "Luther, and Calvin after him, were deeply religious men, and trained theologians to boot, and their revolution took place in the realms of religion and theology. Whatever other effects and tributaries there may have been in the story, that is the point at which to start."[3]

It is indeed the place to begin. For it cannot be said too often that it was not because of what the Reformers *denied* but because of what they *believed* that the Reformation was effected. The Reformation was the result of what Philip Schaff in a memorable phrase described as "a deeper plunge into the meaning of the gospel." Great movements do not live by negations. They certainly include denials and negations but that which empowers and sustains them is their affirmations and their hopes. So the place to begin is in the religious struggle, the fresh apprehension of the gospel that was gained, the place of the basic revolution. This is particularly necessary in the case of Luther. For, as Philip Watson has observed, "It is rarely in human history that anyone appears who will dig down to examine foundations on which...[people] build, and test their soundness."[4] But that is what Luther did. And more than that. Having found the foundations insecure, his greatest achievement was to clarify in a remarkable way the Christian understanding of the basis and the nature of the relationship between God and man.

Here I wish to focus our attention on three things. First, I want to recall for a moment Luther's spiritual struggle. It is an almost inexhaustible human story, of exceptional religious depth and meaning, but I mention it because the themes of Luther's thought that I see as being so important for us today were born out of that struggle. Secondly, I will point to certain characteristics of the contemporary religious and theological scene to which Luther's theocentric faith is particularly relevant. Then, finally, I will explore briefly the social significance of the central affirmation of justification by faith.

I The Relevance of Luther's Spiritual Struggle

By way of approaching our first concern, the question of the significance of Luther's struggle for those themes of his theology which are particularly relevant to our circumstances, we raise the general question of the importance of doctrine in all this. Frequently, when attention is directed to Luther's clarification or reconception of the divine-human relationship, the great importance of *doctrine* for Luther and his heritage is immediately stressed. That is surely understandable. Indeed it is always salutary to remember just how tenacious Luther could be concerning the necessity for right doctrine, how firm was his commitment to truth and with what disdain he would have viewed the theological softness that marks some contemporary movements and Christian apologetics. "For doctrine," Luther asserted in his extended comment on Galatians 5:9, "is like a mathematical point. Therefore it cannot be divided; that is, it cannot stand either subtraction or addition." Nor is he moved by those who accused him and his followers "of offending against love and thus doing great harm to the churches. We are surely prepared," he continues, "to observe peace and love with all men, provided that they leave the doctrine of faith perfect and sound for us. If we cannot obtain this, it is useless for them to demand love from us." The reason is that in a matter of decisive significance, such as the "issue of salvation," when faced with those who "teach lies and errors under the guise of truth" then "love is certainly not to be exercised, and error is not to be approved."[5] Luther was not given to mincing words. Clearly, if one is to be faithful to Luther one must not minimize the significance of doctrine. But it is necessary to pause here. For it is important that the concern for doctrine be not too quickly detached from the spiritual struggle. For Luther also equated true doctrine with the wisdom of the Cross,[6] and such wisdom is not to be gained, or held, without the engagement of the soul with the Christ whose cross it is. The depth and the fruitfulness of his understanding are inconceivable apart from the profound wrestling that marked his quest for a gracious God and the agonies which attended his continuing encounter with Him.

My concern can be simply put. When we discuss the religious revolution set loose by Luther, we do not err in stressing the importance of doctrine, but we can press the point in a wrong way. It was no abstract theological concept, but a powerful experience giving birth to concepts that were revolutionary. It is this which has entered into subsequent generations with such life-giving strength. The creativity lay in the way theology *and* experience, doctrine *and* life had been so vitally joined. A distinguished Biblical scholar of our time has recently paid striking tribute to this creativity. In the Preface to his Commentary on Galatians, Hans Dieter Betz writes: "There is at least one commentary which…expresses an extraordinary and profound understanding of what Paul intended to say: Luther's commentary of 1535. Written after earlier attempts and including the entire range of scholarship available at the time, Luther's commentary is more than a scholarly comment *upon* Galatians. It is a recreation *of* Galatians in the sixteenth century." Then he adds this amazing sentence: "Luther speaks as Paul would have spoken had he lived at the time when Luther gave his lectures."[7] One wonders if there is any other Father of the Church about whom such a statement could be made. But however that may be, it is eloquent testimony to the fact that Luther's theology, the themes of his doctrine, were born from the depths of the spiritual struggle that engaged his whole being.

Luther had as his challenging purpose in the monastery that of effecting a complete contrition before God. Being a man possessed of a lively sense of truth and reality, we understand why he never ceased to distress himself over his sins. Perhaps it should be noted again that Luther, though assuredly not made of wood or stone, was not troubled by carnal temptations and he marvelled that St. Jerome had been so upset by them. Luther was vexed, as he put it, "not about women, but about the really knotty problems" of life. He was troubled about the way man is curved in upon himself, seeking himself not only in earthly good things but even in the things of God; as if at the height of his devotions, the devil were to whisper: "Well done, Brother Martin! Soon you will not need God at all." The really knotty problems circled around the great themes of the drama of redemption—sin, the law, predestination and above all the righteousness of God. That phrase became for him a terrible phrase, representing the unrelenting judgement of God as it reached into every nook and cranny of his being. It formed the context of his temptation to despair, of *Anfechtung,* the experience of "the desperate, guilty isolation of one trapped, condemned, alone beneath the Wrath of God."[8] Love for God should be free, spontaneous, joyful but Luther looking into himself knew, as he put it: "Though I lived as a monk without reproach, I felt that I was a sinner before God with an extremely disturbed conscience. I could not believe that he was placated by my satisfaction. I did not love, yes, I hated the righteous God who punishes sinners ...."[9]

You know the story. Wrestling day and night, beating, as he puts it, "importunately upon Paul at that place" he sees that the "Righteousness of God" is not just the standard by which we are judged, it is the liberating power out of which we live, the gift of grace by which we are justified. He records the experience in words that thrill with the spirit of liberation: "Here I felt that I was altogether born again and had entered paradise itself through open gates." And just as that phrase, that Pauline phrase, "the righteousness of God" which had been such a stumbling block had become "the gate to paradise" so through it "a totally other face of the entire Scripture showed itself to me."[10]

Here indeed was deliverance. Now, he saw with the kind of clarity that comes only from deep experience, that the basis of the relationship with God lay not in our piety or achievements of any sort, but in the spontaneous, unfathomable depth of God's love that reaches us in all our limitations and all our unworthiness. The foundation of life was not some dubious virtue of our own but the inexhaustible love of God, the ultimate reality in all that is. It was a liberating personal experience. But at its heart is a radically theocentric understanding. This theocentric emphasis has been rightly described as the fundamental motif of Luther's thought. This meant that because man has received from God everything which he could bring that, in the words of Paul Althaus, "Taking one's stand before God on the basis of moral or religious achievements would therefore mean nothing less than forgetting that God is God...."[11] But equally it meant that "'it is as great a sin to despair on account of our own unworthiness as to presume on account of our righteousness.'" Both "are symptoms of an anthropocentric attitude to God, which will not let Him be Himself, that is gratuitously good."[12]

Luther had made a discovery that had all sorts of creative consequences. But that was the sixteenth century. The world has undergone drastic changes. His question is certainly not one which grips our age. Indeed Paul Tillich "viewed the contemporary man, and even the contemporary Protestant, as almost constitutionally incapable of understanding Luther's central conception, the doctrine of justification by faith."[13] I shall return to this issue shortly, but first I wish to point to another area where I think the major themes of Luther's thought have peculiar relevance to our contemporary religious and theological scene.

II. Themes Relevant to our Circumstances

One of the most thoughtful and provocative books to appear on the North American theological scene in recent years is the first volume of James Gustafson's *Theology and Ethics,* entitled *Ethics from a Theocentric Perspective.* It is his contention that "religion is increasingly advanced as instrumental to subjective temporal ends...." It is his judgement that "Religious belief, trust and practice, are offered as useful instruments for getting on well in the business of living, for resolving those dilemmas that tear individuals and communities apart, and for sustaining moral causes, whether they be to the right, the left, or in the middle. Both individual pieties and social pieties become instrumental not to gratitude to God, the honor of God, or service of God, but to sustaining purposes to which the Deity is incidental, if not something of an encumbrance."[14] Gustafson sees this not only in those popular contemporary religious expressions in which religion is obviously presented as instrumental to everything from such matters as individual happiness, social success and more satisfactory sexual functioning. We are faced with something that involves not only the superficial but also the most serious religious thought of our day. Man has become not only the *measurer* of all things, which he always is; he has increasingly become the *measure* of all things: "Religion and God have been put in the service of human needs."[15] And Gustafson is concerned that the implications of this whole drift is leading "to a distortion of the place of man in the universe."[16] This anthropocentrism denies the tragic aspects of life and, to use first-order religious language, "implies" also "a denial of God as God—as the power and ordering of life in nature and history which sustains and limits human activity...."[17] He thus thinks we need to attend to a theological tradition which is concerned with "that which is objective in relation to human subjects."[18] Of course he knows and values the "consolations," "inspirations," and "benefits" of religion. His argument is that these "come from a deep spiritual consent to the divine governance ... [and] that the old defect of hubris or pride is the problem that correlates with the failure to give that consent ..."[19] This failure properly to attend to what can be discerned about "the ordering power of the world" and instead to focus so immediately on the concern for happiness, success and fulfillment is theologically and pastorally wrong.

I am in substantial agreement with Gustafson's analysis of our circumstances. Indeed the real evil of this utilitarian attitude is that "it creates a type of piety in which there are no longer any genuine engagements between the soul and God, but merely a religious accentuation of various forms of ethical and political idealism"[20] or the undergirding of accepted cultural values. But this brings us right back to Luther.

Luther calls us to radically theocentric faith. But it is not just the theocentric orientation of his thought that is relevant to our circumstances. It is also its character. Luther's thought about God is thoroughly Christocentric. It is not an abstract objective order to which he points us but to the God who through the Bible had encountered him in the depth of his experience. This God is, as he put it in an unforgettable image, "a blazing oven, all aglow with love" but precisely because His is that, it is a fearful thing to fall into His hands. The message is one of inexhaustible grace, but it is never cheap, because by it we are judged in every aspect of our beings. The theocentric understanding of Luther is anything but remote from our daily existence; on the contrary, it embraces every emotion, every aspect of our lives. Luther thus challenged not only the crass utilitarianism of his day, but dug down to the foundations and laid bare the living Rock of Christian faith. He is a great resource for us.

III. The Social Significance of Justification by Faith

We noted above that Paul Tillich regarded contemporary man as almost totally incapable of understanding Luther's conception of Justification by Faith. Tillich was sure that the concern that so agitated Luther is no longer vital for modern man. We are, he felt, simply "not troubled by any divine demand for righteousness or by any search for a merciful God."[21] The doctrine of justification was, however, still significant, and what was needed was to relate it to man's sense of meaninglessness and the experience of radical doubt. And so Tillich contended, "not only he who is in sin but also he who is in doubt is justified through faith. The situation of doubt, even of doubt about God, need not separate us from God. There is faith in every serious doubt, namely, the faith in the truth as such, even if the only truth we can express is our lack of truth. But if this is experienced in its depth and as an ultimate concern, the divine is present ..."[22]

At about the same time as Tillich was showing the relevance of the doctrine to the religious-intellectual sphere in this fashion, Reinhold Niebuhr was articulating a social and political ethic in terms of the same Reformation doctrine. This was an elaboration or application of the doctrine that is of immense importance for us in the present day. For we are a generation who live daily with tragic choices. And surely the genius of the Christian faith as expressed in the doctrine of justification is that it illuminates the tragic dimensions of life through the same reconciling act of Christ which provides resources to cope with those tragic realities. The resource of insight and spirit articulated in the doctrine of justification thus forms the basis of an ethic that is needed for all political life, filled as such life always is with ambiguity and frequently with tragic choices. Every statesman is daily faced with trying to realize partially incompatible goals. Being responsible often means making the choice of suppressing one value in order to secure or to preserve another. Moreover, the very struggle to secure justice itself involves the use of the instruments of power, and the instruments of power are always ambiguous. Nor can innocence be maintained or purity achieved by withdrawing from the struggle. In a word, *there is no moral hiding place.*

Resolute in his pursuit of justice, but with no illusions about the ambiguous nature of the instruments necessary for that pursuit, Niebuhr put in a concise and memorable way the social meaning of this doctrine: "Justification by faith in the realm of justice means that we will not regard the pressures and counter pressures, the tensions, the overt and covert conflicts by which justice is achieved and maintained, as normative in the absolute sense; but neither will we ease our conscience by seeking to escape from involvement in them. We will know that we cannot purge ourselves of the sin and guilt in which we are involved by the moral ambiguities of politics without also disavowing responsibility for the creative possibilities of justice."[23] Or to put the matter somewhat differently, to act socially in terms of justification by faith is to know two things: 1) it is to know that the Divine love which impels us to seek a greater justice also illumines the sin in which we are involved by our efforts, and 2) this doctrine also assures us of a resource of mercy to cover the evil we do in order to be responsible. This is a perspective that saves us at the same time from both a paralysis of will and the pretension to which our relatively righteous causes usually tempt us. It bids us combine the spirit of resolution against evil with an awareness of "the taint of sin in the cause of our devotion." This doctrine is usually presented and understood in exclusively personal and individualistic terms, but surely the full range of the truth to which it is testifying demands that its significance for social and political life be set forth. Indeed, the meaning and truth of the doctrine, to say nothing of its healing and liberating power, will not be available until it is seen engaging the ambiguity of our political decisions and the tragic dimensions of history.

To illustrate what I mean, I turn to a moment in American religious and social history of the mid-nineteenth century. To read much of the Protestant theology of that period in America, to say nothing of the literature of social and political conflict, is to be left wondering whatever happened to this cardinal doctrine of the

Reformation. It is present, of course. But one has the feeling that it is there because it is supposed to be there. After all, it is an honored part of the heritage and theological discourse would be incomplete without it. But one thing is clear: it is not a doctrine that is informing religious life and thought in a vital way. And surely one of the reasons why it was not doing so is that those who affirmed it failed to bring it into a living engagement with the great social issues of the day. And that was a great pity. For if ever Christians needed whatever resources of insight and healing there are in Christian faith to engage the ambiguous values and tragic choices of communal life, it was that time and place.

As I read the debates of churchmen over the issue of slavery, I keep asking this question: "Would not a living understanding of Justification by Faith have been both illuminating and healing?" I believe it would have, for two reasons. First, the doctrine points to the riches of Divine Love which throws a searchlight into the depths of evil in which we are involved. At the same time it points to the resources of grace enabling us to cope responsibly with a difficult situation. The doctrine really is indispensable for dealing with the tragic choices of life. And therein lies both its truth and its relevance. But it would, I think, have enabled those evangelical Christians to have said: "We know that we are involved in an evil situation. We also know that there is now no easy kind of solution. But we are serious about getting rid of this evil; we will set a realistic timetable to show our resolution, and we know that there are resources of grace to cover the evil in which we will be involved in our attempts to be responsible and just." But they did not say that sort of thing. And the reason was this: moralism had become the content of their Christian understanding, obscuring the depths of both sin and grace. This ingrained moralism meant that they felt they must always be righteous, supporting always righteous causes, instead of being forgiven sinners coping as best they could in an ethically complex situation with an entrenched social evil. The result was most instructive and we have seen similar results scores of times: *Things could no longer be called by their proper names.* So slavery was no longer condemned as an evil, as it had previously been in the South; it was now declared to be a positive good.

Now, I want to stress that we must not feel superior in any way to those Christians of the Old American South. Actually there are few groups so attractive in so many features of their piety. Nor was their failure simply a failure of courage. It was a theological failure. That meant that the depths of both sin and grace, and consequently the meaning of the doctrine of Justification by Faith, were obscured by the all pervading moralism. This meant further that when the conflict was joined in bloody civil war, a rationalistic and moralistic theological understanding, instead of illuminating the tragic dimensions of the conflict, served rather to reinforce and intensify the crusading self-righteous moralism of both sides.

The doctrine of justification does not mean that we do not take sides in the struggle to secure social values. It does not say: "A plague on all your houses." It does not say that "since sin abounds, no significant distinctions are to be made." It is not an invitation to neutrality. No. It does mean that the very faith that impels us to action, also keeps us aware of the fact that our cause, though perhaps relatively righteous, is not absolute. This awareness will not get rid of conflict but it will mitigate the ferocity of the struggles in which we are and must be engaged if treasured social values are to be secured and preserved. And just as the individual before God is kept from being sentimental by the reality of his sin, and from despair by the largeness of God's mercy, so here an ethic shaped by the doctrine of justification promises that combination of realism and hope that is at once the fruit of biblical faith and the perennial need of society.

We began by noting how easily the Reformation could have been engulfed by important secondary causes of various kinds, and that part of the greatness of Luther was that his religious message did not get centred in or swallowed up by them. Here, at the conclusion, I wish to return to that theme.

Luther did not create the revolution known as the Reformation, but he did set it loose. There is no complete answer to the question why he, unlike his predecessors, was able to do this. The relationships between key figures and great historical events is never subject to ready explanation. But some things can be said. Certainly Luther did not succeed simply by articulating his theological understanding in splendid isolation from his world. Indeed, to understand his impact at all, we must see how Luther and his message were related to two powerful currents in his day. The first was the strong, bitter, and long-standing criticism of the church. One brief document puts the situation before us: '"He [the Pope] seems to despise and to impoverish our nation .... Church offices are no longer given to those who deserve them, but to those who offer most for them. In order to raise the money, new indulgences are granted every day .... A thousand ways are thought out by which the Roman See presses the gold out of us with cunning devices, as though we were barbarians.... But now the best amongst us, as though startled out of their sleep, have begun to consider by what means they can deal with this injustice. They are determined to shake off the yoke and to recover their former freedom. Thus the Roman curia will suffer no mean damage, if the princes carry out what they have in mind.' This letter does not come from the early days of the Reformation, but was written sixty years previously, in 1457, from an official of the Archbishop and Elector of Mainz to Enea Silvio Piccolomini, later Pope Pius II."[24] This was one current to which Luther was related.

A second current was more subdued but of equal importance. It was the development, especially in Germany, of a concern for intense personal piety. This "religion of quiet inwardness" represented a new religious vitality that was to prove to be of large importance for the Reformation. Gerhard Ritter has seen more clearly than most the relationship of Luther to these two currents: "In retrospect we see both currents of church opposition at work simultaneously though at first independently. The one struggles against manifest abuses and insists on reforms, but in practice does not go beyond a patchwork improvement of institutions. Though it does not reach down into spiritual depths, it is nevertheless most · impassioned, impelling, and popular. The other current is less concerned with the outward appearance of the church, but instead touches on the substance of religion and the spiritual roots of Church life.... In the figure of Martin Luther the two currents combine for the first time. He is a man of the people, an agitator in the grandest style...he uses all the slogans of anticlerical and antipapal opposition of the preceding hundred years and still out does them—but at the same time he is the most brilliant and profound theological thinker, the most powerful and strong-willed prophet-figure of his people, and a religious genius whose experience of faith is of unprecedented inwardness and intimacy.

This combination is plainly unique. And thus Luther became incomparably the most formidable opponent of the Old Church.''[25]

We can add, this was the combination that had the power to set loose a revolution, without becoming engulfed in it.

Genius can never be emulated and in any event ours is a vastly different situation. Nevertheless, in our time also, two important currents of religious life which belong together are frequently divorced, or at best are running parallel to each other. There is, on the one hand, the concern for personal piety and renewal that somehow does not see that words like "justice" belong with "forgiveness" and "repentance" in the Christian life. On the other hand, there is a passionate, almost professional social concern which is surely right, but which frequently lacks the guidance and depth that can be provided by the central doctrines of the faith. Until these two dimensions are united, Christian life and witness will suffer impoverishment. They belong together. But they cannot be brought together by asserting the validity of each in turn. Our task is to see the way they *are* together in the centre of the faith and to draw out the meaning of that for the full range of personal and social life. Our task is a theological task, but one that involves not only professional theologians, but the whole church. A full elaboration of the social significance of the doctrine of justification by grace could form a significant beginning on this agenda. Deep theological digging in this centre, so powerfully clarified by Luther, holds out a promise of renewal. It would also be a fitting celebration of this anniversary.

ENDNOTES

1. Jaroslav Pelikan, "The Enduring Relevance of Martin Luther 500 Years after His Birth," *The New York Times Magazine* (September 18, 1983):43.

2. Gordon Rupp, "Martin Luther, 1546-1946," *The London Quarterly and Holborn Review,* vol. CLXXI, Sixth Series, 15(1946):108-109.

3. G.R. Elton, *Reformation Europe 1517-1559* (London: Collins, 1963), pp. 274-275.

4. Philip S. Watson, *Let God be God: An Interpretation of the Theology of Martin Luther* (Philadelphia: Muhlenberg Press, 1950), p. 63.

5. Lectures on Galatians 5:9, WA 40,II:46:25-27, 47:23-25, 48:18-21; LW 27:37-39.

6. Walther von Loewenich, *Luther's Theology of the Cross* (Minneapolis: Augsburg Publishing House, 1976), p. 23.

7. Hans Dieter Betz, *Galatians: A Commentary on Paul's Letter to the Churches in Galatia* (Philadelphia: Fortress Press, 1979), p. xv.

8. Gordon Rupp, "Luther and the German Reformation to 1529," in *The Reformation 1520-1559*, 2:73, *The New Cambridge Modern History* (Cambridge University Press, 1958).

9. Preface to Latin Writings, WA 54:185:21-24; LW 34:336.

10. WA 54:186:1-2, 4, 8-10; LW 34:337.

11. Paul Althaus, *The Theology of Martin Luther* (Philadelphia: Fortress Press, 1966), p. 123.

12. Watson, p. 135.

13. James Luther Adams, "Paul Tillich on Luther," p. 307, in Jaroslav Pelikan, ed., *Interpreters of Luther: Essays in Honor of Wilhelm Pauck* (Philadelphia: Fortress Press, 1968).

14. James M. Gustafson, *Ethics from a Theocentric Perspective* (Chicago: The University of Chicago Press, 1981), p. 18.

15. Ibid., p. 83.

16. Ibid., p. 83.

17. Ibid., p. 84.

18. Ibid., p. 84.

19. Ibid., p. 20.

20. Reinhold Niebuhr, *Essays in Applied Christianity* (New York: Meridian Books, 1959), p. 95.

21. Adams, p. 315.

22. Paul Tillich, *The Protestant Era* (Chicago: The University of Chicago Press, 1948), p. xiv.

23. Reinhold Niebuhr, *The Nature and Destiny of Man* (New York: Scribner's, 1943)2:284.

24. The quotation and comment are taken from Gerhard Ebeling, *Luther: An Introduction to His Thought,* trans. by R.A. Wilson (London: Collins, and Philadelphia: Fortress Press, 1970), p. 59.

25. Gerhard Ritter, "Why the Reformation Occurred in Germany," *Church History* 27 (June, 1958):106. Translated from the original "Kirche und geistiges Leben in Deutschland um 1517," (ch. 8 of the author's *Neugestaltung Europas im 16 Jahrhundert*, Berlin, 1950) by G.H. Nadel.

II LUTHER: EXEMPLAR OF REFORM— OR DOCTOR OF THE CHURCH?

by
Harry McSorley

To speak of Luther as a theologian for Catholics and Protestants requires qualifications in order to safeguard historical and theological truth and, consequently, to provide a firm—that is, a historically and theologically sound—basis for restoration of full communion among Christians. Such a qualified reception of Luther may help offset any unjustified euphoria accompanying the perfectly justifiable spirit of positive appreciation that has been voiced in virtually every room of the Christian household on the occasion of the fifth centenary of Luther's birth. Moreover, it is only through an assessment of Luther that is both critical and fair that one will dispel the notion that ecumenical theology itself is some kind of "romantic" enterprise.[1]

I shall introduce this assessment of Luther by pointing out in part I in a rather general way some of the senses in which he is *not* a theologian for all Christians, not even for all Lutherans. This will lead to a more specific examination, in section II, of a sense in which Luther does not seem ecumenically "receivable"— namely, as a model or exemplar of church reform. The path will then be clear for us to look in part III at the positive way in which Luther can serve both Protestants and Catholics today as a "common doctor" who can help them bring about that which he was unable to do—the restoration of unity between the Roman Catholic Church and the churches resulting from the Protestant reformation.

I.

Luther was clearly not a theologian for such Catholics as Pope Leo X, who first censured, then excommunicated Luther. Nor was he a theologian for such Catholic adversaries as Prierias, Eck, Cochlaeus and their twentieth century heirs, Denifle, Grisar and Maritain.[2] There were also critical Catholic humanists who wanted reform, but not in Luther's manner.

Neither was Luther a theologian for those fellow reformers whom he called "Anabaptists" and worse to the extent that he and they refused to accept the position of the other on such matters as infant baptism, the permissibility of images and traditional liturgical forms. Nor was he a theologian for Zwingli and his followers, and the Calvinists, to the extent that each side found the eucharistic theology of the other unsatisfactory. A considerable portion of English Protestantism also balked at Luther's sacramental theology.[3]

Luther is not even a theologian for all Lutherans in the important sense that only three of his hundreds of works, the *Catechisms* and the *Smalcald Articles*, have been received into the normative Lutheran collection known as the *Book of Concord*.[4] When Luther's other writings are drawn upon in the *Formula of Concord*, the final part of the *Book of Concord*, the qualification is made that the Holy Scripture is the sole rule and norm of all doctrine and that even Luther's writings are subject to it.[5] Here we have embedded in the official Lutheran confessions an important qualification concerning the manner in which Luther's theology is to be regarded by Lutherans. To accept all of Luther's theology without subjecting it to a scriptural critique is un-Lutheran![6] When the *Formula of Concord* was taking shape in the late 1570s, strong Lutheran pressure was exerted to limit the number of Luther's works that were to be received officially because of the problems that arise when "human writings" are set alongside "the Word of God."[7]

The official or formal reception of Luther's works by Lutherans is even more restricted when one considers that many Lutheran churches—those of Denmark, Norway and France, as well as some of the smaller non-European Lutheran churches—do not include in their constitutions the *Formula of Concord* with its limited reception of Luther's writings.[8] Among these churches Luther's Catechism, sometimes more specifically his 'Small Catechism', is often but not always singled out as a secondary interpretative norm along with the *Augsburg Confession*.[9] There are, then, some Lutherans who do not put *any* of Luther's works on the same level as the *Augustana*.

The rather formal facts mentioned in the two previous paragraphs disclose a deliberate attitude of critical reserve and sobriety towards Luther even among those who link their form of Christian life with his name. With this attitude Lutherans have thus heeded well Luther's own critical view of his work.[10]

II.

"I have said more than once: Let anyone attack my person however he will. I don't claim to be an angel!"
WA 7:275:1-2 (*Against Emser*, 1521)

I am not going to accept Luther's invitation to "attack his person." I intend, rather, to raise some questions about Luther's justification of an aspect of his personal behaviour that many Christians, not just Roman Catholics, still regard as an obstacle which prevents them from recognizing the father of the reformation as an exemplar of church reform "for all seasons." The barrier of which I speak is Luther's polemical manner of reviling and disparaging his "opponents," be they Roman Catholic "papists" (to use the most mild epithet he hurled at them), Protestant "enthusiasts," "fanatics," "sacramentarians" or "false brethren," or Jews and "Turks."[11] I shall take it for granted that the average reader knows what I am talking about and that I need not rehearse examples of Luther's invective. For those who wish a quick review, Luther's 1543 treatise against the Jews and his 1545 tract against the papacy are generally regarded as the low points of his verbal abuse of those deemed by him to be in the power of Satan. It also goes without saying that Luther was not the only master of the art of verbal assault in the sixteenth century, nor was his anti-semitism any greater than John Eck's. But no one is proposing Eck or Cochlaeus as theologians for Catholics and Protestants! Nor do they have the kind of place in Roman Catholicism that Luther has in Lutheranism and in Protestantism.

Before his excommunication Luther could confess with apparent sincerity, though not without some persuasion by the Roman emissary, Charles von Miltitz, that he had spoken the truth too heatedly and too sharply and had gone too far in his criticism of the Roman Church.[12] Despite the hard-hitting tracts of 1520, Luther followed the advice of his friends and of his prince-protector and assumed a reserved posture at the Diet of Worms in 1521.[13] He soon regretted having been mild there when he should have spoken out like a prophet.[14] The "civil" criticism of the church made by Erasmus, Capito and others, which abstains from "chiding, biting and giving offense", accomplishes nothing, argues Luther, for the pontiffs thus think they can continue in their ways uncorrected.[15] His "reprehending" of papal and ecclesiastical abuse and false teaching will thus become increasingly sharp and vituperative, culminating in the tracts of the 1540s mentioned in the preceding paragraph.

The acerbity of Luther's polemic, especially that directed against the papacy, has alienated Roman Catholics from the sixteenth century to the present, including such relatively irenic interpreters as Joseph Lortz, Albert Brandenburg and Cardinal Jan Willebrands.[16] In a recent study of Luther's critique of the papacy which, in my judgement, fails to bring out that Luther's critique was conditional, not absolute,[17] Scott H. Hendrix points out, as did Karl Holl,[18] that Luther was able to find some precedent for his offensive speech in the language of the prophets and even in that of Jesus and Paul.[19] Moreover, contends Hendrix, it was Luther's conscientious conviction that the papacy was doing serious harm to the church—and not some ''abysmal hatred''—that led him to his passionate critique of the papacy.[20]

I find this, at least to some extent, a plausible line of explaining, if not excusing, Luther's polemical behaviour. It also seems to me that the view articulated by Melanchthon in his oration at Luther's funeral, and embraced most recently by both Mark U. Edwards Jr.[21] and Hendrix,[22] is also a just and ecumenically appropriable way of interpreting and relativizing Luther's hard-line polemics. While refusing to dispute the observation made in his day even by people who were ''not evil'' that Luther was harsher (*asperior*)than he ought to have been, Melanchthon responded with a sentiment he said Erasmus had spoken often: That, in view of the magnitude of its ills, God has given this age a severe physician (*acrem medicum*).[23] Not just Erasmus, but other Catholics such as Eck, Pope Adrian VI, and speakers at the Council of Trent, even if they did not offer positive assessments of Luther's teaching, could also see God chastising the church through Luther.

Melanchthon himself seems to be granting that Luther's harsh style of reform is not the remedy for the less glaring reforms of which the church constantly stands in need.[24] For one reason, as Luther himself foresaw and then acknowledged after the fact: his reformation had about it a tragic dimension,[25] a division of the Western church that has proliferated and persisted.[26] But there is another reason. Precisely because the ecumenical movement of our age is showing signs of becoming God's instrument in overcoming Christian discord, Christians are going to have to think together about the way a future ''church uniting and reforming'' is continually to be open to reform and renewal. This justifies us in looking a bit more deeply at some of the rationale Luther used to justify his polemic mode of reform so that we can distance ourselves from it, while remaining open to what he has to say to us as a common teacher.

Were God so to have intervened at Luther's death as he did at Lazarus', I think Luther would have leaped from his coffin to denounce Melanchthon for suggesting that he had spoken too harshly against his opponents. By what standard did Melanchthon and other good people then and later regard Luther's polemic as offensive? By the standard of Christian love, of course, especially as the radical implications of that standard were disclosed by Jesus in the Sermon on the Mount. This critique of Luther's harshness ignores the hard fact, however, that Luther did not think he or any Christian preacher was bound by those standards when confronted with enemies of the Gospel.

As Luther proceeded on his course of sharp opposition to the Roman Church, he consistently exempted parents, preachers and public officials from the command of Mt. 5:22—not to be angry with our brother or call people names—when they are exercising their "office" or acting as "public persons."[27] By 1545 the exception extends to *all* Christians as Luther asks: "Should not I as a Christian, and should not all lovers of our Lord Christ rightly be impatient, angry and intolerant, and moreover curse the ac cursed papacy and call it the most shocking names, a papacy which is not ashamed to blaspheme our Lord most disgracefully and turn his promises into lies?"[28]

Nor, for Luther, does the command to love our enemies, to bless those who curse us, to do good to those who hate us and pray for those who persecute us in Mt. 5:44 apply to those in the preaching ministry or to other public persons when they are acting as such.[29] In this sermon Luther first states without qualification that the Christian person "shows no hatred nor enmity whatever toward anyone and has no anger in his heart—only sheer love, gentleness and kindness, just as our Lord and His heavenly Father do, whom he here even offers as an example."[30] But why is it, asks Luther, that so many holy people in the Scriptures curse their enemies, even Christ and his apostles?[31] "Or how can I love the pope, whom I daily rebuke and curse, and rightly so?" The answer, says Luther, is that "the office of preaching is not ours, but God's. But what is God's is not our doing, but his, through the Word and ministry as his own gift and activity. But since it is written in John 16 that it is the office of the Holy Spirit to reprove the world ... He cannot just tell the world what it wants to hear, but must rebuke it and speak sharply against evil."[32] Luther sums up his interpretation of Mt. 5:44 by saying: If someone interferes with our love and service of God, "neither love nor service applies to him, since the text says: 'You shall love and do good to *your* enemy.' But I must be an enemy to *God's* enemy so that I do not rise up with him against God."[33]

The great Luther scholar Paul Althaus takes note of the distinctions and the exceptions Luther makes when dealing with the love requirement of the Sermon on the Mount, yet makes the astonishing claim that "Luther does not weaken the Sermon on the Mount in the slightest. He accepts it in its full rigor."[34] It would seem truer, I think, if Luther's name were to be added to the long list of those who, as Guenther Bornkamm puts it after reviewing the history of exegesis of the text, have sought to interpret the Sermon on the Mount by trying "to limit its validity."[35]

Gordon Rupp, the renowned Methodist Luther scholar, is confident that he is expressing the attitude of virtually all his fellow British Free Churchmen when he rejects Milton's view that Luther's animosity on behalf of his great cause should be ranked among the Christian virtues.[36] Many of Luther's own followers then[37] and now[38] have found his polemical manner offensive. In 1970 the Lutheran World Federation in fact seized the opportunity presented by Cardinal Willebrands' historic positive statement concerning Luther[39] to make history itself by formally repudiating the sub-Christian aspects of the reformation polemics. Since that statement does not seem to have received the publicity it deserves, I take the liberty of citing it here:

"It is ... in accordance with [the] commandment of truth and love that we as Lutheran Christians and congregations be prepared to acknowledge that the judgment of the Reformers upon the Roman Catholic Church and its theology was not entirely free of polemical distortions, which in part have been perpetuated to the present day.

"We are truly sorry for the offense and misunderstanding which these polemic elements have caused our Roman Catholic brethren. We remember with gratitude the statement of Pope Paul VI to the Second Vatican Council in which he com municates his plea for forgiveness for any offense caused by the Roman Catholic Church. As we together with all Christians pray for forgiveness in the prayer our Lord has taught us, let us strive for clear, honest and charitable language in all our conversations."[40]

In closing this critique of Luther's polemical manner, justice requires that attention be drawn to at least one great moment in his career when Luther demonstrated that he could identify with a style of reformation writing that was markedly different from his own. I refer to his attitude toward the *Augsburg Confession*, the great unifying document of virtually all Lutheranism. In the doctrinal section of the *Augustana*, even though several "Anabaptist" doctrines are condemned, no dogma of the Roman Catholic Church is attacked. More important for the point of this section is the fact that the *Augustana* is free of Luther's characteristic polemic. We thus have a reception of Luther's key reformation insights along with a non-reception of Luther's polemical style by the most authoritative utterance of the Lutheran reformation. This analysis by no means advocates an ecumenism at the expense of Luther,[41] but rather a reformation theology which overcomes that which most Catholics and many Protestants think is the most objectionable aspect of Luther's reformation—its polemical style. That Luther, too, was capable of disengaging his reformation teaching from the polemical armour and assault weapons with which he surrounded it, is evident from the fact that, despite some early grumblings, Luther was able not only to embrace en-thusiastically the content of the *Augustana*,[42] but also to point with pride at its irenic character![43] The latter point provides further evidence that Luther's comments about Melanchthon's "soft-pedalling" (Leisetreterei) during the Diet of Augsburg was meant not as a rebuke but as a genuine compliment.[44]

III.

"... but I will let no one attack my doctrine without responding, because I know that it is not mine, but God's." WA 7:275: 3-5(*Against Emser*, 1521)

Having criticized the less than angelic manner in which Luther carried out his reform, we are now in a position to see him as a teacher for Protestants and Catholics. One more caveat is needed, however. When Luther says his teaching is not his, but God's, it should be clear from what has been said in the first section that this refers to that teaching of Luther which is in conformity with the Scriptures. Luther certainly did not exempt himself from his own canon: "The saints have often sinned in their own lives and erred in their writings, but the scriptures cannot err ... [Therefore] nothing is more dangerous than the works and the lives of the saints which are not grounded in the Scriptures."[45]

With that guideline in place, I can proceed to mention some basic ways in which Luther can serve as a teacher for all Christians. Then I shall single out certain of Luther's teachings which I think are particularly appropriate today, first for Protestants, then for Roman Catholics, from the point of view of Christian reconciliation.

In his funeral oration for Luther, Melanchthon listed several teachings of Luther that, in his mind, represented a blessing for the whole church. I think it fitting to mention them and in the order Melanchthon chose: In the first place, Luther was one who overcame the "very obscure" teaching in the church of his day about "penitence" by unfolding a doctrine of "true penitence" which pointed to the One who is the source of our first spiritual consolation in the face of anxiety about God's judgement. Luther showed the distinction between law and gospel and between the "justice of the Spirit" and civil justice. He taught the true invocation of God based on faith and a good conscience, an invocation directed to the one Mediator, the Son of God, sitting at the right hand of the Father interceding for us. He ennobled civil life by showing that it, too, is pleasing to God. He separated necessary works from ceremonies, rites and laws that impeded the true invocation of God.

35

His German translation of the Bible was of such clarity that its readers derive more light from it than from a number of commentaries. His own commentaries, as even Erasmus admitted, excelled by far those of previous authors.[46] Can any Christian, Catholic or Protestant, who is to any extent conversant with Luther's teaching on the above matters, as well as with Luther's German Bible, fail to agree with Melanchthon that "the light of the Gospel has been made to shine more brightly by the voice of Luther?"[47]

The list of those aspects of Luther's theology that have gained, or deserve to gain ecumenical acceptance can be considerably lengthened. I wish to use the remaining space, however, to suggest some ways in which Luther's theology has been heard and still might be heard by Protestants and by Catholics so as to facilitate reform and reconciliation among the still separated churches of the West.

A. **Luther: A Theologian for Protestants**

The ecumenical movement of our time has given rise to a new appreciation of the sacraments by Protestants, at least, but by no means exclusively, on the level of theology and church leadership. This does not represent some kind of latter-day catholicizing of Protestantism, but rather the recovery of evangelical and catholic substance that is integral to the New Testament and to the reformation theology of Luther, Calvin and other reformers. It does represent the overcoming of one of the most baleful effects of what might be crudely called "enlightenment" theology, which introduced into Protestant thought a disastrous disjunction between "word" and "sacrament," to the detriment of the latter. No one can study the theology of the Father of the Reformation, or Calvin for that matter, and conclude that Protestantism is a church of the "word" and Catholicism a church of the "sacrament."

Accompanying this new awareness that sacraments are integral to Christian life are strong signs that Christians are on the way to concord in the matter of baptism, the Lord's supper and the ministry to a degree that is without precedent since 1520. This rapprochement includes the prospect of surmounting the historically ugly division between at least some of the heirs of those who, in the sixteenth century, were uncharitably and unjustly called "Anabaptists" and virtually all other Christian churches. Historic divisions between Lutherans, Catholics, Calvinists and Baptists concerning the sacrament of unity, the Eucharist, also appear to be in the process of being overcome as a result of prayerful, sustained dialogue and study between previously estranged members of the Christian household.[48] Luther's voice has been appropriately heard in all these discussions, along with other Christian voices, and the central thrust of his teaching has had a significant impact on the emerging consensus on the sacraments.

I draw attention here to Luther's teaching on both Baptism and the Eucharist mainly to point to something else to which it is intimately related that is just beginning to find a place on the ecumenical agenda: the importance of "right teaching" and the doctrine of infallibility. Just as one cannot read Luther and fail to see that the sacraments were integral to the original form of Protestantism, neither can one read him carefully and overlook the centrality of right—and inerrant—teaching for his theology. The development of Protestantism into so-called "Orthodoxy" followed by "Pietist," "Enlightenment" and "Liberal" reactions to it, turned much of Protestantism away from something that was at the very heart of Luther's teaching, a concern for true doctrine. Some of those who admired him for diverse reasons from the eighteenth century to the present have even seen in Luther's critical stance toward the canonicity of biblical books grounds for first criticizing and then rejecting the Christian articles of faith concerning the divinity of Jesus, the Trinity and other articles of the creed—in the name of Luther![49] The popular consequence of this radical "Protestant" critique of the Christian faith is that the ordinary Protestant in the nineteenth and much of the twentieth century assumed a stance of doctrinal tolerance if not indifference, while seeing Catholics as "dogmatic." This was an exact reversal of the roles which Luther saw being played by himself, on the one hand, and the Catholic, Erasmus, on the other during their historic exchange. The "new" Protestants, who wanted to be extremely reticent in making doctrinal assertions were thus on the side of Erasmus, while the Catholics were found offensive because they were (unwittingly) following Luther's injunction: "not to delight in assertions is to cease to be a Christian."[50]

Just as Luther's realistic sense of the sacraments has been a stimulus, although certainly not the only one, in helping contemporary Protestants to regain their Reformation's sacramental roots, so also Luther's appreciation of doctrine and of ecclesial infallibility may help overcome post-Reformation Protestant attitudes that render difficult the dialogue with Roman Catholics on the question of ecclesial and papal infallibility. Protestant-Catholic discussion about papal infallibility is often in difficulty at the outset because those on the Protestant side do not share with their Catholic partners the belief that the whole visible church, that is, the church that baptizes infants and celebrates the Lord's Supper, is in any meaningful sense infallible. Here it is where Luther might be of help. For the ''founder'' of Protestant Christianity firmly believed in the infallibility of the church and its ''articles of faith.'' Included in these ''articles'' is the Christian legitimacy of the practice of infant baptism and the true, sacramental presence of the body and blood of Jesus Christ in the Lord's Supper.

When his various biblical arguments on behalf of infant baptism failed to have effect, Luther could say quite confidently: ''All of Christianity from East to West has baptized infants for more than a thousand years .... Because the church is holy, if it had erred it would not be holy.''[51] This kind of argument throws light on what Luther understands by a scriptural proof. Obviously clear biblical warrant is desirable. But even if such evidence is not available, if there is a universal Christian practice that is not opposed to Scripture, this is a strong indication that it is right.[52]

In the debates over the true presence of Christ in the Eucharist, Luther was convinced he had a ''clear'' biblical proof for the traditional doctrine. Nonetheless he did not hesitate to appeal to the fact that this doctrine was an article of faith held by the whole church, as is attested by the writings of the Greek and Latin Fathers and by daily ''use'' right up to his time:

"[Such] testimony of the entire holy Christian Church (if we had nothing else) ought of itself [allein] be sufficient for us to abide by this article .... For it is dangerous and dreadful for us to hear or to believe contrary to the united testimony, faith, and doctrine of the entire holy Christian Church as it has unanimously taught from the beginning for over fifteen hundred years .... Whoever doubts [this article], in effect, does not believe the Christian Church. Such a person not only condemns the entire holy Christian Church as a damned heretic, but also Christ himself with all the apostles and prophets, who have given the basis and the powerful testimony for this article that we confess: "I believe one holy Christian Church" .... One may trifle with paper or imperial laws or other human tradition of the Fathers or councils, but not with articles of faith which have been with us from the beginning and which have been unanimously upheld throughout Christendom."[53]

This scratching of a relatively untapped mine of Luther's theology already enables us to conclude that: (1) the concept of the inerrancy of the whole church, often called ecclesial infallibility, is integral to Luther's evangelical-catholic reformation theology,[54] (2) the "holy Christian Church" of which Luther speaks in *this* connection is not some invisible reality (except in the sense that, as an object of faith we believe it and do not "see" it) but the very concrete church that baptizes babies, celebrates the eucharist and studies the Bible. (3) It is erroneous to say, with Adolf von Harnack that Luther's critical scriptural principle brought to a close the history of dogma, for this overlooks the crucial truth that Luther felt bound not only by God's Word, but also by the divinely grounded and sustained articles of faith which mediated that Word to him and which led him to interpret Scripture in the light of those articles. Just as Luther invoked the inerrancy of the "entire holy Christian Church" against opponents of his day, so too, *per impossibile*, would he have invoked the same principle against "neo-Protestants" from the enlightenment through Harnack and beyond who thought that in the name of Luther's critical scriptural principle they could discard this or that article of the faith of the whole Christian Church. This overlooks a core aspect of Luther's theology: ecclesial inerrancy.[55] (4) Recovery of this basic reformation doctrine of the inerrancy of the entire church will surely facilitate dialogue on the question of conciliar[56] and papal infallibility which can only be understood as instruments and signs of the basic inerrancy of the whole church.

B. **Luther: A Theologian for Catholics**

Luther has long been a theologian for Roman Catholics, though this has seldom been acknowledged. For example, although some of the disciplinary reforms at the Council of Trent may have been thinkable apart from Luther—viz., the dissociation of almsgiving from indulgences, provision for proper education and discipline of the clergy, the crucial requirement that bishops be pastors of but one diocese and reside in it—it is quite unlikely that they would have been enacted without Luther's prophetic exposure of the harm done to the church by the lack of such reforms. Luther's central doctrinal concern, the doctrine of justification by faith through grace, and its corollary, the unfreedom of the sinner to do anything for justification apart from the liberating grace of Christ, was unquestionably heard and appropriated by Trent, even though, to be sure, in its own idiom.[57]

The similarity between some key aspects of Luther's theology and that of the Second Vatican Council is also discernible—even if his name is not found in the footnotes to the council documents! One thinks here of the council's teaching on the primacy of the Word of God over all of church life; the attendant recognition that the teaching ministry in the church is not above God's Word, but ministers to it; the fostering of a biblical piety in the church, the use of the vernacular in the liturgy as one aspect of an overall reform of the eucharistic liturgy; emphasis on the preaching of the Gospel as integral to the duties of the ordained ministry; restoration, albeit only on a limited basis, of the chalice to the laity, elaboration of a fuller doctrine of the priesthood of all believers than one can find in even the *Book of Concord*; situation of papal primacy and infallibility within the context of the whole church and of episcopal collegiality, thereby overcoming a serious deficiency caused by the unanticipated adjournment of Vatican I; recognition that reform of both church doctrine and discipline are necessary; and finally, the very crucial acknowledgement that the one church of Christ extends beyond the boundaries of the Roman Catholic Church.[58]

The last point is one that accords fully with Luther's view of the church and its inerrancy. A doctrine or a practice that has been held by the entire holy church, if it is in harmony with Scripture, is, for Luther, inerrant. But if such a doctrine or practice has only been received by part of the church, can it be required of the whole church if it does not seem to be clearly in conformity with Scripture? The implications of this particular point of Vatican II's and Luther's teaching seem to me to be far-reaching, though as yet little-appreciated by Catholic theologians. Does not such a doctrine require Roman Catholics to do some retroactive thinking? Are the Western councils of the second millenium truly ecumenical if they did not involve or have not yet been received by the rest of the church?[59] If they are not, this does not automatically mean everything they said was false. But it would give Roman Catholics some flexibility in deciding upon the authoritativeness of the various doctrines taught by all those councils, something which could bode well for Christian reunion.

There are many other aspects of Luther's theology which might still be heard with profit by Catholics. On the occasion of the anniversary of the Diet of Worms, for example, a representative group of Catholics from that city requested Pope Paul VI to issue a clarifying word about Luther that would take into account the findings of recent Catholic Luther scholarship, in a fuller manner than Cardinal Willebrands had done the year before at the assembly of the Lutheran World Federation. This would not only serve the cause of justice, they said, but would also make it easier for Catholics to follow those parts of Luther's theology that are cherished by many Christians of all confessions. They cited Luther's theology of faith, his insights into biblical interpretation, his doctrine of sin and of the paradoxes of the Christian life, his doctrine of the hiddenness of God and "what is perhaps most important, his theology of the cross."[60]

Each of these themes could become the object of reflection, but I shall resist that urge and draw attention to still another point, or complex of points, where Luther's theology still needs to be heard by Catholics as they undergo internal renewal in preparation for reconciliation with other Christian churches. I refer to Luther as the doctor par excellence of Christian liberty.

If Protestants can derive from Luther a renewed sense of reverence for the Church's "articles of faith," Catholics have much to learn from him about "unity in necessary things, liberty in doubtful thing," a principle to which Vatican II subscribed. The Roman Catholic Church has just promulgated a new code of canon law at a time when Lutheran and Anglican theologians are beginning to see the desirability of a universal Petrine ministry exercised by the Bishop of Rome, provided Christian liberty be safeguarded.

How central the question of canon law is for Christian reunion can be gathered by simply recalling: (1) it was the canon law procedures in force in Luther's day that provided the machinery for his excommunication; among other things, the law required retraction from Luther rather than fraternal dialogue, and it allowed such avowed, literally prejudiced opponents of Luther as Eck and Prierias to be involved in forming the judgement against him; (2) it was the canon law text of his day that Luther sent to the flames in 1520 along with the papal bull threatening his excommunication.

Christian liberty, as Luther expounded it, does not mean that there is to be no canon law or any discipline in the church. Indeed, as early as the great treatise *On Christian Liberty* of 1520, Luther warned against those, who, as soon as they hear of the liberty of faith, turn it into a fleshly liberty, thinking that if they believe, they are now permitted to anything they like. "They want to show they are free Christians only by despising and rejecting ceremonies, traditions and human laws."[61]

We cannot find in Luther nor derive from his works a new canon law. In fact, Luther confessed that the question of church ordinances was "the most difficult question of all, variously addressed by many, but actually settled by no one."[62] In many quarters of the Roman Catholic Church, particularly among canon lawyers, there is an appreciation of the fact that all church discipline and law must reflect the Gospel of Christ if it is to be worthy of the Christian people. It is quite doubtful that the new code, in all respects, measures up to that norm. To the extent that it does not, one can also be confident that when the *next* revision of the code is undertaken, the evangelical insights of Luther will play a significant role.

Closely related to Christian liberty, if not one of its components, is loving, loyal, yet courageous criticism of church leaders, pronouncements, preaching, worship, and structures whenever these obscure the gospel, impede the mission or infringe Christian liberty. Whether he was speaking sarcastically or whether it was through uncharacteristic lack of imagination, the only way Luther could see a Christian minister responding to ecclesiastical abuse, if he were bound by the Sermon on the Mount, is as follows:

"Am I to say to our enemies, the Pope, the bishops, princes and whomever, who persecute the gospel and trample on the people who hold on to it: Dear lords, may the dear God reward you. You are pious people and holy fathers, etc., or should I keep silence, show them reverence, or kiss their feet etc.? I am a preacher who ought to have teeth in his mouth, to bite them and irritate them and to tell them the truth, and if they don't want to hear it, to excommunicate them, to bar them from heaven, to send them to hell's fire and give them to Satan for God's sake, etc."[63]

Surely the way of Jesus lies between these extremes of dishonest, fawning flattery on the one hand and verbal assault on the other. Is it not the Christian standard to be watchful, to stand firm in the faith, to be courageous and strong, while at the same time letting all that we do, including reproving, rebuking and other occasionally painful acts of church discipline, be done in love?[64]

One of the key factors contributing to the rise of an uncritical attitude toward the papacy on the part of many Catholics was precisely the unbridled criticism hurled at it during the reformation. This Catholic over-reaction on behalf of the papacy, as distinct from the theological case for the Petrine ministry that is gaining ecumenical acceptance in our day, has probably contributed as much to the continuance of Christian division as has the excessively critical rejection of the papacy by the reformation.

Luther was not uncatholic in criticizing the one who held the place of Peter. There have been Catholic precedents since the rebukes to Peter administered by Jesus and Paul. Thomas Aquinas, for example, says, to the objection that it is not proper for a subject to admonish a prelate: "To argue with and to scold *irreverently* is prohibited, but he can admonish *charitably* as Paul did to Peter in Gal. 2:11."[65]

One may justly ask: where were these "charitable admonishers" during the scandalous period of the church in which Luther found himself? Luther soon learned that his "reverent" attempts at reform were getting nowhere. In fact, they only seemed to incite vituperative responses, which unfortunately drove him to reply in kind, thus giving rise to the tragic and sinful dimensions of what had originally been a Catholic reform of the church. Five hundred years after his birth Catholics are increasingly coming to see Luther as a "beloved preceptor," not just for Protestants, but also for themselves. And they will increasingly be able to appropriate even the image of Luther as the courageous and conscientious reformer when that image is purified and itself reformed by the principle: "in all things, charity." For, as Luther has written, "God's Ten Commandments ... demand obedience not only of kings and emperors, but also of prophets, apostles, and all creatures." That includes, I would add, reformers as well.

ENDNOTES

1. Steven E. Ozment, *The Reformation in the Cities* (New Haven and London: Yale University Press, 1975), pp. 5 and 169, note 18, applies this term to the impressive ecumenical studies of Hans Kueng and Otto Pesch. If Kueng's book on Karl Barth's doctrine of justification is "romantic," so is Barth's acknowledgment that Kueng has understood his thought *exactly*. To call Pesch's rigorously argued thousand-page study of Luther and Aquinas on justification "romantic" is surely to redefine that term. It is, moreover, not true that the conclusion of Pesch's work is that Luther and Aquinas are "saying the same thing in different ways." For Pesch they are often saying *really different* things as a result of a basic opposition in their very understanding of the nature of theology. Even where there are unbridgeable differences between the two—this is Pesch's main point—these differences ought not to be seen as church-dividing: *Die Theologie der Rechtfertigung bei Martin Luther und Thomas von Aquin* (Mainz: Matthias Gruenewald Verlag, 1967), pp. 941-948, 950, conclusion 4; cf. pp. 529 and 537-552, 885-890.

   Three things might be said about Ozment's verdict, pp. 3-4, that the very title of my own book, *Luther: Right or Wrong?* (New York and Minneapolis: Paulist Press and Augsburg Publishing House, 1969), expresses "the strong apologetic undercurrent" of the "Lortz school": 1) I do not belong to that "school"; 2) the title for the American edition was chosen by the *Lutheran* co-publisher; 3) those who read the sub-title, which *is* mine, will see that it is not an exercise in apologetics, but in ecumenical theology, the unromantic nature of which is explained at length by Heinrich Fries in the foreword to the American version.

   Heiko A. Oberman, *Luther: Mensch zwischen Gott und Teufel* (Berlin: Severin und Siedler, 1982), p. 325, shows little awareness of what actually goes on in ecumenical dialogues when he insinuates that they "pass over in silence those questions which separate Christians."

2. One cannot say with equal ease that Luther was not a theologian for the Council of Trent. See my essays "Luther, Trent, Vatican I and Vatican II," *McCormick Quarterly*, 21(1967):95-104, and "Luther and Trent on the Faith Needed for the Sacrament of Penance," *Concilium*, 61(1971):89-98. At Trent no less a person than the future Pope Urban VII had to point out that Luther and Calvin taught many things that were true, including their agreement with St. Jerome's teaching that the distinction between bishops and priests is the result of a church decision, not divine precept, S. Ehses, ed., *Concilium Tridentinum* (Freiburg: Herder, 1965) 2nd ed., 9:54:25-39.

3. See B.A. Gerrish, "John Calvin on Luther," and William A. Clebsch, "The Elizabethans on Luther," in Jaroslav Pelikan, ed., *Interpreters of Luther* (Philadelphia: Fortress Press, 1968), pp. 67-96 and 97-120.

4. *Formula Concordiae*, Solida Declaratio, Von dem summarischen Begriff, 6:9, in *Die Bekenntnisschriften der evangelisch-lutherischen Kirche* (Goettingen: Vandenhoeck & Ruprecht, 1959), 4th ed., pp. 836-837. Henceforth cited as B S L K. Cf. Theodore G. Tappert, trans. and ed., *The Book of Concord: The Confessions of the Evangelical Lutheran Church* (Philadelphia: Fortress Press, 1959) § 9, p. 505. Henceforth cited as Tappert.

5. B S L K, p. 837, lines 3-16 (Latin). The text states that this critical view of Luther's works comes from Luther himself! S D, Rule and Norm, § 9, Tappert, p. 505.

6. Hubert Jedin's admonition, "Whoever wants to make all of Luther Catholic, becomes a Lutheran himself," implies a standard for "being Lutheran" that is foreign not only to the *Book of Concord* but also to Luther. "Zum Wandel des katholischen Lutherbildes," p. 46, in H. Gehring, ed., *Martin Luther: Gestalt und Werk* (Karlsruhe: Badenia, 1967). In prefaces to collections of his works in 1533 (WA 38:133f.) and 1539 (WA 50:657-658; LW 34:283-284), Luther sincerely laments that his works are being collected because precious time will be spent studying them instead of Scripture.

7. B S L K, p. 837, note 1.

8. Hans Weissgerber, "The Valid Confessional Symbols," pp. 1-22, in Vilmos Vajta and Hans Weissgerber, eds., *The Church and the Confessions* (Philadelphia: Fortress Press, 1963).

9. For example, the Lutheran churches of Denmark, Norway, Brazil, Bolivia, Ethiopia, the Sudan, Hong Kong, and Taiwan; cf. Weissgerber, pp. 9-11, 15-21.

10. In addition to the texts mentioned in note 6 above, WA 58,I:79-84 provides dozens of citations attesting Luther's genuine humility in criticizing his own writings. See also Karl Holl, "Luthers Urteil ueber sich selbst," in his *Gesammelte Aufsaetze zur Kirchengeschichte* (Tuebingen: J.C.B. Mohr, 1923) I:398-401, 2nd and 3rd ed; English trans. by H.C. Erik Midelfort in Jaroslav Pelikan, ed., *Interpreters of Luther*, pp. 20-22.

11. For a survey of Luther's polemical style, see Bernhard Lohse, *Martin Luther: Einfuehrung in sein Leben und sein Werk* (Muenchen: Beck, 1981) pp. 91-96. Miriam Usher Chrisman, "From Polemic to Propaganda: The Development of Mass Persuasion in the Late Sixteenth Century," *Archive for Reformation History*, 73(1982:175-196, offers evidence which helps us see how second-generation "propagandists" tore asunder the seamless garment of Christ that had only been ripped by earlier "polemicists." However, by restricting the term "polemic" to "a controversial argument" which "connotes a two-way ... dialogue, although it may be a dialogue between the deaf" and excluding from it any "systematic attempt to propagate a particular opinion or doctrine [whose] purpose is to influence men's opinions and thus their actions and behaviour," which, following L. Doob, she calls "propaganda," p. 175, she thereby disjoins things that were, at least in Luther, intimately related, if not indistinguishable. Mark U. Edwards, Jr., *Luther and the False Brethren* (Stanford, Calif.: Stanford Univ. Press, 1975), carefully analyzes the polemical exchanges between Luther and the Protestants who disagreed with him. His introduction and conclusion, however, contain insufficiently grounded assertions about the allegedly different nature of the polemic between Luther and the Catholics of his day. For example, as will be shown in the next section, Luther, too, could argue "from Scripture and tradition as interpreted by the church"; cf. Edwards, pp. 1-2. Furthermore, in view of the collection of texts assembled in WA 58,I:136-137 about Luther's reference to himself as a prophet, it is incorrect to say that "he made no special claim about himself" to Catholics, but only to Protestants, ibid., p. 2.

12. WA Br 1:290:20-22, 29; 293:42-44; LW 48:98 and 102 (letter to Elector Frederick and draft of a letter to Leo X, Jan. 5 or 6, 1519).

13. Richard Friedenthal, "Hier stehe ich ... Luther und das Lutherverstaendnis," pp. 60-72, in Fritz Reuter, ed., *Luther in Worms: 1521-1571* (Worms: Norberg, 1973). Though he speaks of "Roman tyranny" in his famous speech at Worms, Luther still acknowledges that he was more acerbic than was fitting in his replies to its defenders, cf. WA 7:834:5-6; LW 32:111.

14. WA Br 2:387:5 - 388:25; LW 48:306-307 (letter to Spalatin, Sept. 9, 1521). For similar texts, see Holl, pp. 409-417; English trans. by Midelfort in Jaroslav Pelikan, ed. *Interpreters of Luther*, pp. 25-30.

15. WA Br 2:387:16 - 388:1; LW 48:306-307. According to Luther it was the pope, not he, who first resorted to unpeaceful tactics: WA Br 2:245:15-16; LW 48:192 (letter to Spalatin, Jan. 14, 1521).

16. For references to Lortz and Brandenburg, see Remigius Baeumer, *Martin Luther und der Papst* (Muenster: Aschendorff, 1970), 2nd ed., p. 99. In his historic address to the Lutheran World Federation, after giving what amounts to the first official, positive Roman Catholic pronouncement on Luther's person and teaching, Willebrands used rhetorical silence to express the depth of Catholic feeling on this point: "It is a consolation for me to think that we share the same sentiments if in these joint reflections I prefer to say. nothing about certain particularly sharp attacks that Martin Luther made against the Roman Pontiff; they sadden my heart and I feel sure that you, too, regard them as a burden," p. 64 in LaVern Grosc, ed., *Sent into the World: The Proceedings of the Fifth Assembly of the Lutheran World Federation, Evian, France, July 14-24, 1970* (Minneapolis: Augaburg Publ. House, 1971). I can only agree with Otto Pesch in his magnificent book *Henfuehrung zu Luther* (Mainz: Matthias Gruenewald Verlag, 1982), when he applauds the way in which Willebrands is able to speak of Luther as "our common teacher" (cf. the German text in H.-W. Heszler, ed., *Evian 1970* [Witten, Frankfurt, and Berlin: Eckart, 1970], p. 99) and when he calls for a more extended application of this term to Luther's teaching, ibid., pp. 272-279. But in view of the words of Willebrands cited above and in terms of the critique that I offer in this section, I cannot agree with his recommendation: "Don't worry about [Luther's] sharp polemic! One may read this as a reflection on the conditions in the church of his day and as the angry expression of a deep suffering in respect to the church!" ibid., p. 279. As we shall see, Luther's polemic involves more than this.

17. See my essay, "Luther's Ecclesiological Significance for the Twentieth Century Ecumenical Movement," *The Springfielder*, 35(1970):131-139, and Harding Meyer, "Das Problem des Petrusamt in evangelischer Sicht," in Karl Lehmann, ed., *Das Petrusamt* (Muenchen and Zuerich: Schnell & Steiner, 1982), pp. 110-125, esp. pp. 119-121.

18. Holl, p. 414; English trans. by Midelfort in Jaroslav Pelikan, ed., *Interpreters of Luther*, p. 28.

19. Scott H. Hendrix, *Luther and the Papacy* (Philadelphia: Fortress Press, 1981), pp. 152-156. Luther's invocation of St. Paul in his 1531 *Lectures on Galatians* as a model for his own polemics is presented at length, but without critical comment, by Edwards, pp. 112-126. Theological critique is necessary, however, when we are looking at Luther from an ecumenical perspective. For the moment I simply put the question, with respect to the later *Lectures on Galatians,* whether Luther truly reflects the standard of Jesus when he teaches that "charity can sometimes be neglected without danger" or that, in defense

of the Gospel, "charity is certainly not to be exercised toward those who teach lies and errors": WA 40,II:48:12-13, 18-21; cf. 47:22-28; LW 27:38-39. On the different behaviour that is alloved "according to faith" and "according to charity" see WA 40,I:188:12-15; LW 26:103; cf. WA 40,I:193:20-194:12; LW 26:107. Highly important, by way of contrast with the kind of behaviour Luther elsewhere defends for himself and urges on others, is Luther's acknowledgment here that Paul "does not inveigh against Peter sharply, but treats him with sufficient reverence": WA 40,I:193:14-15; LW 26:106.

20. Hendrix, pp. 152-156. Lohse, p. 194 speaks of Luther's "unimaginably deep hatred of the papacy."

21. P. 205.

22. P. 152.

23. *Corpus Reformatorum,* ed. C.G. Bretschneider, Halle: Schwetschke, 1843, 11:729.

24. Second Vatican Council, *Decree on Ecumenism,* n. 6.

25. WA Br 2:388:35-39; Satan is trying to cause a dreadful tragedy in Germany (letter to Spalatin, Sept. 9, 1521); LW 48:307-308. Tetzel was "the primary author of this tragedy": WA 54:184:31-32; LW 48:335 (preface to his Latin works, 1545). Cf. WA 51:541:7-9 (*Against Hanswurst,* 1541); LW 41:234.

26. Muentzer formed the first "sect," Carlstadt, the second, the Baptists, the third. Luther predicts many more sects will arise after his death, "God help us": WA TR 5:49:15-50:3 (October, 1540). Cf. WA 40,I:681:3-9 (Galatians, 1535); LW 26:455.

27. WA 45:112:8, 12, 13 (Sermon on Mt. 5, July 8, 1537): "Ibi semper excipiendus magistratus die mussen zurnen....Ideo [being angry] est virtus apud magistratum et etiam Christianos in officio, in parentibus." Cf. WA 17,I:242:1-243:24; LW 12:194; WA 20:455:37-456:15; WA 34,II:6:19-8:27.
   Luther's concern in making these exceptions is that evil not go unpunished. The exception is also allowed for the same reason in his otherwise restrained treatment of the 5th and 8th commandments in the *Large Catechism:* WA,I:157:34-35; 172:3-5; cf. B S L K 606:21-27; 629:25-30; Tappert, op. cit., 389, 182, 401-402, 274.

28. WA 54:262:12-16; cf. LW 41:331 (against the Roman Papacy). Hendrix, p. 155 cites this passage without referring to the exegetical principle by which Luther justified such polemics.

29. WA 32:397:26-407:4 (Sermon on Mt. 5:43-48 of 1532); LW 21:118-129.

30. WA 32:398:17-20; LW 21:119.

31. He cites Mt 23:13; Acts 7:51; 13:10 and the "anathema" of Gal. 1:8; WA 32:398:31-37; LW 21:119-120. Whether Jesus occasionally "neglected" to practice charity (see note 19 above) or saw himself exempt in his preaching ministry from the demands of his own Sermon on the Mount is a question on which New Testament scholars may be able to enlighten us.

32. WA 32:398:25-31; LW 21:119.

33. WA 32:400:19-23 (my emphasis); LW 21:122.

34. *Die Ethik Martin Luthers* (Guetersloh: Guetersloher Verlagshaus Gerd Mohn, 1965), pp. 68-84, my trans. from his pp. 69-70. *The Ethics of Martin Luther*, trans. by Robert C. Schultz (Philadelphia: Fortress Press, 1972) pp. 62-78 and p. 64.

35. *Jesus von Nazareth* (Stuttgart: Kohlhammer, 1956), p. 204. More recent studies of the Sermon on the Mount by Lutherans either do not mention Luther's interpretation—John H. Elliott, "Law and Eschatology: The Antitheses of the 'Sermon on the Mount,'" *Lutheran World*, 15(1968):16-24—or mention it briefly and only in connection with the opening it has provided for later Lutherans to be too passive(!) in the face of abuse by the "worldly regiment": Leonhard Goppelt, "Das Problem der Bergpredigt," in Goppelt, *Christologie und Ethik* (Goettingen: Vandenhoeck & Ruprecht, 1968), pp. 28-43, esp. 34-35. Pesch, *Hinfuehrung*, pp. 237-240 and 322-323 likewise raises questions about Luther's exemption of public life from the requirements of the Sermon on the Mount, but does not touch the problem caused by exempting "preachers" from it when they are defending the Gospel. See above note 16.

36. Gordon Rupp, "Luther auszerhalb des Luthertums: Freikirchliche Sicht," *Concilium*, 12 (1976):509. This is coupled with the hope that the polemic of Luther and Milton may be relegated to the distant past, along with other old, unhappy battles.

37. Ernst Bizer, *Luther und der Papst* (Muenchen: Chr. Kaiser Verlag, 1958), p. 47, Edwards, p. 205.

38. Baeumer, p. 99 lists Peter Meinhold and K.G. Steck among the Lutherans who have distanced themselves from Luther's polemic.

39. See note 16 above.

40. "Statement on the Visit of Cardinal Willebrands" adopted by the Fifth Assembly of the Lutheran World Federation, 1970, in Grosc, pp. 156-157.

41. Cf. Peter Manns, "Zum Vorhaben einer 'katholischen Anerkennung der Confessio Augustana': Oekumene auf Kosten Martin Luthers?" *Oekumenische Rundschau* 26 (1977):426-450 and Vinzenz Pfnuer, "Oekumene auf Kosten Martin Luthers?" *Oekumenische Rundschau"* 27 (1977):36-47.

42. *For references in Luther see Pfnuer, p. 43 and Gottfried Krodel's editorial note in LW 49:345-347.*

43. WA 30,III:278:17-279:7 (*Warnung an seine lieben Deutschen*, 1531). Here Luther contrasts the violent behaviour of "the papists" at Augsburg and elsewhere, as well as that of Muentzer and his followers previously, with the peaceful conduct of his followers at the Diet. Christian history, he says, has seldom seen "such a confession, such humility and such patience" as the Lutherans showed at Augsburg. WA 30,III:278:33-35. Cf. Luther on Psalm 118(1530): WA 31:129f.; LW 14:75.

44. See the essays by V. Pfnuer and Heinz Schuette in Joseph Burgess, ed., pp. 8-9 and 52, *The Role of the Augsburg Confession: Catholic and Lutheran Views* (Philadelphia: Fortress Press, 1980). This is clearly the case in Luther's letter of May 15, 1530 to his Elector, WA Br 5:319:5-9; LW 49:297-298. For the more difficult letter to Justus Jonas of July 21, 1530, WA Br 5:495:6-12, see Pfnuer, "Oekumene auf Kosten Martin Luthers?" pp. 42-43.

45. WA 8:485:19-21; 527:16-18; LW 36:137 and 186 (*On the Misuse of the Mass,* 1521). Cf. WA 8:413:17-20; 449:17-18.

46. *Corpus Reformatorum,* 11:728-729.

47. Ibid., 11:728.

48. Cf. *One Baptism, One Eucharist and a Mutually Recognized Ministry: Three Agreed Statements,* Faith and Order Paper No. 73 (Geneva: World Council of Churches, 1975) and *Baptism, Eucharist and Ministry,* Faith and Order Paper No. 111 (Geneva: World Council of Churches, 1982).

49. That story has been told by several authors, among them Ernst W. Zeeden, *Martin Luther und die Reformation im Urteil des deutschen Luthertums,* vol. 1 (Freiburg: Herder, 1950). This study and its accompanying volume of further documentation can still be read with profit without subscribing to the author's view, popular then with Roman Catholics *and* liberal Protestants, that there are in Luther two unintegrated principles, an objective one, that of the traditional orthodox faith, and a subjective one, that of the authority of the critical, free conscience, the latter being responsible for the rise of liberal Protestantism. See the important critique by Ernst Wolf, "Martin Luther und die Prinzipien des Protestantismus in katholischer Sicht," *Theologische Literaturzeitung* 76 (1951): 271-276. See also the chapter on the history of Luther interpretation in Lohse, op. cit., pp. 209-246.

50. WA 18:603:11-12; LW 33:19-20 and the entire contest, WA 18:603-605; LW 33:19-24 (*On the Unfree Will,* 1525).

51. WA 27:52:15-22 (Sermon on the Sexagesima Sunday afternoon, Feb. 16, 1528). For similar texts see Paul Althaus, *Die Theologie Martin Luthers* (Guetersloh: Guetersloher Verlagshaus Gerd Mohn, 1962), pp. 307-309; *The Theology of Martin Luther,* trans. by Robert C. Schultz (Philadelphia: Fortress Press, 1966), pp. 359-362.

52. WA 26:155:29-35 and 168:40-169:2; LW 40:241 and 257 (*Concerning Rebaptism,* 1528). In the same work, WA 26:167:19-35; LW 40:255, Luther argues similarly that the universal reception of the Apostles' Creed as well as of the Bible itself points to God's preservative action. See Jaroslav Pelikan, *Spirit Versus Structure* (New York: Harper & Row, 1968), pp. 87-93 and "Luther's Defense of Infant Baptism," pp. 209-212, in Carl S. Meyer, ed., *Luther for an Ecumenical Age* (St. Louis: Concordia, 1967). That the "faith of a child" used in LW 40:255 to translate "den kinder glauben" of WA 26:167:29 more likely should be translated as "the Apostles' Creed" is clear from such references as WA 41:156:26-30; WA 51:513:5 and LW 13:296, note 59 by Jaroslav Pelican.

53. WA 30,III:552:3-553:10 (*Sendschreiben an Herzog Albrecht von Preuszen,* 1532). Althaus, *Die Theologie Martin Luthers,* p. 326 (English trans., p. 386) offers other texts

which show that "articles of faith" not only are grounded in the Scriptures and confirmed by the universal reception of the church, but also serve to guide our reading of Scripture—even to the point of allowing us to depart from the simple and direct meaning of the words of a biblical text. See also WA 18:700:31-35; LW 33:162—if the literal sense of Scripture clashes with an article of faith, the text is to be interpreted figuratively. Cf. WA 18:707:12-708:18; LW 33:172-174. Luther's critical, biblical principle was thus not an antidogmatic principle as Roman Catholics—and "new-Lutherans"—before and since Adolf von Harnack have thought. In view of the texts to which we have drawn attention, it would seem to be perfectly Lutheran and Protestant, as well as Catholic, to see the reception of "articles of faith," and, indeed, of the "Biblia" itself by the Eastern and Western churches as a sign of God's preservative action in his "Holy Christian Church" which "cannot err": WA 51:515:11 and 30, 518:13-17, 30-34; LW 41:215 and 217 (*Against Hanswurst*,1541). The context of the latter set of references (WA 51:510-519, esp. 512:17-513:12; LW 41:212-219) and also the text of WA 30,III:351:1-16 (*Glosse auf das vermeinte kaiserliche Edikt*, 1531) show that Luther can argue from the inerrancy of "die heilige kirche," which teaches the Word of God, and from the practice of the universal church—"der gantzen Christlichen kirchen"—against erroneous practices or teaching of a particular church.

These Luther references as well as those in the previous two footnotes are simply not taken into account by Gerhard Ebeling, *Dogmatik des christlichen Glaubens* (Tuebingen: J.C.B. Mohr, 1979)1:30-32, when he undervalues the role played by the articles of faith and ecclesial infallibility in reformation theology. One ought not to allow the fact that Luther had no *developed* thought on dogma as a norm of exegesis—cf. Jaroslav Pelikan, *Luther the Expositor* (St. Louis: Concordia Publishing House, 1959), pp. 126-128, 258—obscure the fact that dogma indeed played a normative role in Luther's exegesis.

54. Similar views can be found in Calvin, in sixteenth century English and Scottish divines, as well as in Balthasar Hubmaier's *Catechism*.

55. Like Ebeling (see note 53), Walther von Loewenich, *Luther und der Neuprotestantismus* (Witten: Luther-Verlag, 1963), pp. 404 and 429 muffles the voice of Luther that we have heard concerning ecclesial inerrancy when he says with reference to the traditional Christological and Trinitarian dogmas: for Luther, the thought of their centuries-long ecclesial acceptance had had "only secondary importance."

56. Councils, for Luther, are "the highest judges and the greatest bishops under Christ" for defending "the ancient faith and the ancient good works in conformity with Scripture": WA 50:606:3-7; LW 41:121-122.

57. See note 2 above.

58. Cardinal Willebrands in his Evian address, p. 63 (see note 16) asked: "Is it not true that the Second Vatican Council has even implemented requests which were first expressed by Martin Luther...?" Cf. O. Pesch, *Hinfuehrung*, pp. 151-153 and 217-221; for the way in which Pesch sees Luther as "common doctor" see pp. 272-279. For some of the ways Vatican II modified the Vatican I teaching about papal primacy and infallibility, see my essay "Some Forgotten Truths About the Petrine Ministry," *Journal of Ecumenical Studies*, 11(1974):208-236.

59. See my essay mentioned in the preceding note, pp. 234-236.

60. "Das Wormser Memorandum" in *Luther in Worms*, p. 183, and note 7.

61. WA 7:69:26-31; 70:3-7; LW 31:372. That Luther constantly—and not just in an allegedly later 'neo-papist' period—lamented that his followers confused Christian liberty and carnal liberty is documented by W. von Loewenich, "Die Selbstkritik der Reformation in Luthers Grossem Katechismus," *Von Augustin zu Luther* (Witten: Luther Verlag, 1959), pp. 269-293.

62. Cf. WA Br 5:529:1-3 (enclosure to a letter to Melanchthon, August 3, 1530) and the related correspondence. For Luther's nuanced approach to canon law, see Jaroslav Pelikan, *Spirit Versus Structure* (New York: Harper & Row, 1968), pp. 98-112.

63. WA 32:402:3-11; LW 21:123-124 (Sermon on Mt. 5:44, 1532).

64. Cf. I Cor. 16:13-14 and 22; II Tim. 4:2.

65. *S. Thomae Aquinatis Super Epistolas S. Pauli Lectura*, ed. R. Cai (Rome: Marietti, 1953)2:161, n. 193 on Col. 4:17. For other examples, see my essay mention in note 58, pp. 216-217.

66. *Against Hanswurst:* WA 51:557:4-5 and 21-23; LW 41:247 (1541).

III THE DIVINE COMEDY OF A REFORMATION PRINCIPLE: LUTHER, THE ANABAPTISTS AND BONHOEFFER ON *SOLA FIDE*

by
Harry Loewen

On October 31, 1943, Dietrich Bonhoeffer wrote to his parents from his Tegel prison cell: "Today is Reformation day, a feast that in our time can give one plenty to think about. One wonders why Luther's action had to be followed by consequences that were the exact opposite of what he intended, and that darkened the last years of his life, so that he sometimes even doubted the value of his life's work."[1] In this letter Bonhoeffer goes on to explain that Luther wanted unity of the church, a free society and a genuine social order, but that the results of Luther's work were indifference, licentiousness, insurrection, and "the gradual dissolution of a real cohesion and order in society."[2] Bonhoeffer wonders whether

Luther would have acted differently had he foreseen the results of his work. Reffering to another great Lutheran of the previous century, Bonhoeffer writes: "As long as a hundred years ago Kierkegaard said that today Luther would say the opposite of what he said then. I think he was right—with some reservation."[3]

James Woelfel writes about this letter that it is "fairly clear that Bonhoeffer means that if Luther could have returned in the nineteenth or the twentieth century and seen what had happened to his central ideas, he would have had to switch his emphasis to those facets of his interpretation of the totality of Christian experience which had precisely required *de*-emphasis in the sixteenth century. Both Kierkegaard and Bonhoeffer sought to do just that."[4]

Bonhoeffer was a serious student of Martin Luther, interpreting the Reformer for twentieth-century German society. In his writings, particularly in his *The Cost of Discipleship,* written in the 1930's, Bonhoeffer dealt particularly with Luther's central theological position, justification through faith, and applied this Reformation principle to concrete situations in his own time. In doing so Bonhoeffer not only re-interpreted Luther's doctrine of *sola fide,* but he also moved beyond Luther. Whether Luther would have taught justification by faith differently after seeing the consequences of his theological position is most unlikely; that Luther would have questioned and even dismessed such Lutherans as Kierkegaard and Bonhoeffer as enthusiasts, fanatics, and heretics, is fairly certain.

In this paper I wish to argue that it was Luther's doctrine of *sola fide* which led not only to "cheap grace" among his followers but also to the alienation between the Reformer and those individuals and groups, particularly the Anabaptist-Mennonites, who were at first attracted to Luther and his reformation work but later had to withdraw because they understood Luther's reformation principle in the same way that Lutherans like Dietrich Bonhoeffer were to understand it some 400 years later. Thus in the first part of my paper I shall deal with Luther's understanding of justification by faith and its results among Luther's followers. In the second part a brief analysis of the Anabaptists' position with regard to justification will be presented. In the last part of my paper I shall deal briefly with Bonhoeffer's reinterpretaion of Luther's *sola fide* and show that in trying to bridge the gap between Luther's justification principle and the need for discipleship, Bonhoeffer, while remaining a Lutheran, moves away from Luther's central doctrine and with regard to the grace-works debate places himself within the Anabaptist tradition.

I. Luther's Justification by Faith

At the basis of Luther's work as a reformer lies his spiritual struggle leading to his conversion and his experience of the grace of God. This is not to say that social, political, religious, and economic factors prepared and influenced the course of the Protestant reformation in general and of Luther's work within the framework of that reformation in particular. But it is to say that Luther's activity as a reformer, including his opposition to indulgences, his reformation writings, his translation and interpretation of the Bible and his struggle against radical reformers, including the Anabaptists, cannot be properly understood without recognizing the agony of his spiritual quest and the theology which emerged from it.

When Luther as a young man entered the monastery he hoped to find a gracious God. For some reason, however, Luther failed to solve his inner conflicts, no matter how much he tried to observe the prescribed rules for dealing with such conflicts. As Heinrich Boehmer writes: "The one thing ... that distinguishes Luther from the great mass of ascetics is simply the fact that all the means of quieting such doubts provided for by the old monastic teachers not only failed but rather had a completely opposite effect; that is, they merely increased his inner distress and anxiety."[5]

In his 1535 commentary on Galatians Luther reflected on his years in the monastery. While devoting himself to fasting, vigils, prayers, the reading of masses, and other disciplines, he fostered mistrust, doubt, fear and hatred.[6] For Luther Christ was a fear-inspiring judge, sitting on a rainbow and ready to pronounce judgement upon wicked sinners. Luther feared Christ more than the devil, he wrote in 1537; he could not call upon his name and could not even bear to hear his name mentioned.[7]

Luther's inner breakthrough occurred in 1513 or 1514 when he prepared for lectures on the biblical books. He tells us that while reading the Old Testament prophet Habakkuk, he was struck by

Chapter 2:4: ''The just shall live by his faith.'' From this statement Luther concluded that spiritual life must be derived from faith and that all human attempts, however sincere, to find forgiveness of sins and peace of mind were altogether useless. According to Luther, God imputes his righteousness to sinful man without man's participation in any way, solely on account of Christ's substitutionary suffering and death.

It would be wrong to imply that with his experience of God's grace Luther had discovered something which the medieval church had not known. On the contrary, the Catholic church had a highly developed doctrine of grace.[8] But the difference between the Catholic understanding of grace and Luther's experience was that while the church had the power to bring down the grace of God through such channels as the sacraments, the Reformer experienced God's grace directly, without, as he put it, ''the works of man.''

Luther's sense of having grasped the full truth concerning man's redemption by the grace of God and through faith alone was so strong that he came to identify his doctrine with the heart of the gospel.[9] To the end of his life the doctrine of justification by faith was for Luther the sum and substance of the Word of God, the centre of theology, the basic truth of Christianity, the theological article by which the church would stand or fall. Those who opposed him, did not oppose Luther but the gospel of Christ.[10] To Chancellor Brueck Luther wrote confidently that his cause was God's cause and that God could never forget those who had made God's cause their own.[11] According to Luther, only those who understood and taught justification by faith could be considered true theologians.[12] Time and again Luther stressed that if the article of justification were lost, all Christian doctrine would be lost as well. People who do not believe in justification by faith, Luther quipped, are either Jews, Turks, papists, or heretics.[13] According to Luther, no salvation was possible without believing in justification by faith. In 1522 when he preached his famous eight sermons to restore order in Wittenberg, Luther asserted repeatedly that while God had chosen him to be the instrument of much needed reform, it was *God* who worked for renewal and not he. While he was drinking beer with his friends in Wittenberg, Luther said, God reformed the Church.[14] And in the 1530's Luther stated: ''This is the reason why our theology is certain: it snatches us away from ourselves and places us outside ourselves."[15]

Luther's critics have charged that the Reformer carried a "protestant tone" into his version of the German Bible. To underline his doctrine of justification by faith Luther inserted the word "allein" (alone) in Romans 3:28 in spite of his friends' advice against it. Those New Testament books which seemed to contradict the doctrine of justification by faith, Luther did not regard as fully inspired. The Epistle of James in particular, an "epistle of straw", as Luther called it, was a stumbling block for the Reformer because it stressed the importance of "works" in addition to faith.[16] Luther did not regard the Book of James as the writing of an apostle, because James was against St. Paul and all the rest of Scripture in ascribing justification to works.[17] Luther did not think it possible to reconcile Paul and James. If someone could bridge the two positions for him, Luther challenged his table companions, he would consent to being called a fool.

Since Luther had found the answer to his spiritual anguish in the Bible, it followed that Scriptures, as understood and interpreted by him, became his absolute authority in matters of faith. Early in his career Luther believed and taught that all Christians should be allowed and encouraged to read and interpret the Bible for themselves and apply its message to their faith and life. In this Luther believed that all readers of good will and led by the Holy Spirit would not only find the gospel, that is justification by faith in the pages of the Bible, but also come to understand all important biblical truths as he understood them.[18] When such radical reformers as Andrew Carlstadt, Thomas Muentzer, and the Anabaptists claimed the principle of the priesthood of all believers for themselves as well, and interpreted the gospel contrary to the Reformer's understanding of it, Luther was certain that he was right, and that those who contradicted and opposed him were not only wrong but also of the devil.

With his discovery of the principles of "sola fide" and "sola scriptura", Luther's path as a reformer became more and more clear. The late medieval reformers who had wished to reform the church "in head and members," had been more concerned about abuses and the moral corruption in the church than its dogma and theology. Luther, on the other hand, intended to reform the *theology* of the church rather than its morals. In dedicating his booklet *The Freedom of a Christian* (1520) to Pope Leo X, Luther wrote that he had no dispute with anyone concerning ethics but only concerning the word of truth, by which he meant justification by faith.[19] When he appeared before the emperor and the church officials in Worms, Luther stressed that his concern was the gospel and not the morals of the church. In 1521 he wrote to some of his Catholic opponents: "Whether you are good or bad does not concern me. But I will attack your poisonous and lying teaching which contradicts God's word."[20] Luther stressed time and again that he would have had little to do with the papists had they taught the Word of God correctly; their sinful life was of little concern to him. In his Table Talks of 1533 Luther is reported as saying: "Doctrine and life must be distinguished. Life is bad among us, as it is among the papists, but we don't fight about life and condemn the papists on that account .... I don't scold myself into becoming good, but I fight over the Word and whether our adversaries teach it in its purity."[21]

In all his early writings and sermons Luther emphasized the grace of God and human impotence with regard to salvation. In his lectures on Romans Luther stressed, to be sure, both justification through faith and striving after righteousness, but he left the door open to a misunderstanding and perversion of the principle of justification by stating that it is better to remain in one's sins than becoming overanxious about human failings.[22] In his 'Heidelberg Disputation" of 1518 Luther elevated the "Grace of God" above the "Law" and the demands of God. Not only the works of men stand in the way of God's grace, Luther argued, but the law of God itself "cannot advance man on his way to righteousness, but rather hinders him."[23] In his pamphlet *Two Kinds of Righteousness*, written in 1519, Luther distinguishes between an "alien righteousness," which comes to the individual by grace; and another, "our proper righteousness," which is the product of "alien righteousness" and is its fruit and consequence.[24] This comes close to saying that "alien righteousness" will of necessity result in man's "proper righteousness", that is, faith will result automatically in good works. In his *Treatise on Good Works* (1520), which was prompted by the concern of his followers that Luther's emphasis on justification would lead to a disregard of good works,[25] Luther argues in favour of good works and fruits of righteousness, provided that these works are the result of faith: "... good works ... are not good in themselves, but must be done in faith and in the assurance of God's favour ..."[26]

In 1520 Luther wrote his major reformation works in which he attacked the Roman Catholic Church and developed his theology. In one of these writings, *The Babylonian Captivity of the Church,* Luther reduces the seven sacraments to two - baptism and Holy Communion—largely on the basis that the sacramental system was, according to him, the work of men. It is significant to note that Luther retains the "real presence" of Christ in the eucharist but rejects the sacrificial nature of the mass primarily because in the celebration of the mass the human role remained too pronounced. Luther denied the human role in the eucharist, believing that Christ was present in the elements without the action of the priest. In the presence of God man is completely passive, according to Luther; he simply accepts what Christ freely offers him. According to Bornkamm, Luther retained Christ's "real presence" in Holy Communion and rejected the sacrificial nature of the mass because he yearned for "a reality of grace not less real than his sins. His doctrine of Holy Communion is an expression of his faith in this reality of God in the midst of the world's reality ... and his belief in the reality of forgiveness."[27]

Similarly in his book *Against the Celestial Prophets - Concerning Images and the Sacrament* (1525) Luther argues that such radicals as Carlstadt and Zwingli have misunderstood the great truth concerning the eucharist because they have not experienced the forgiveness of God.[28] And a gracious God can only be experienced by faith, a faith which, according to Luther, the "sacramentarians," including the Anabaptists, did not accept.

Luther's major work, *On the Bondage of the Will* (1525), written against Erasmus the humanist, must also be understood in the light of his central doctrine of justification. Luther rejected free will on the ground that for him it is God who is the real cause of all events and actions and that it is God—not man's virtues or sins—who wills man's salvation.

Luther's doctrine of justification by faith also determined his understanding of baptism. The sacrament of baptism was for Luther another channel through which God bestowed grace and favour upon sinful man. While Luther in his early writings expressed doubts concerning the validity of infant baptism, he later argued, especially after the Anabaptists appeared, that in the baptism of infants justification by faith was most effectively exemplified. Particularly in infant baptism Luther came to see more and more a means of *receiving* the grace of God. Little children, Luther explained, cannot boast of having done anything to acquire God's gracious forgiveness; they simply receive freely what God offers them.

In 1528 Luther was asked about the beliefs and practices of the Anabaptists with regard to baptism. In an open letter entitled *Concerning Rebaptism,*[29]Luther finds occasion to answer this question and to address the subject of baptism more fully than he had done before. Luther argues that to baptize upon an individual's confession of faith, as the Anabaptists teach and practice, is ridiculous, for how can one be certain whether the baptismal candidate believes or has faith? Such a baptism is nothing more than a "baptism of adventure." One should not baptize upon a person's confession of faith but on the basis of the Word of God, that is, upon the Bible's command to baptize. Moreover, Luther asks, how can the Anabaptists be sure that children have no faith? Is it not possible for Christ to implant saving faith in the hearts of infants? The leaping of John the Baptist in his mother's womb when Mary the mother of Jesus visited Elizabeth was surely a sign of his faith. Infant baptism is, in fact, most biblical, Luther argues, for little children are not required to exert any kind of effort on their part or do any kind of good work with regard to their salvation—they are free, sure, and blessed through the glory of their baptism.[30]

Not only did infant baptism exemplify for Luther the passivity of man and God's redeeming act in salvation, but it also assured Luther that in the sacrament of baptism his sins were forgiven on the basis of God's Word and not because he had done anything to deserve the favour of God. Jaroslav Pelikan observes correctly when he writes: "Luther could console himself with his baptism in hours of temptation, defying the devil with the cry 'Baptisatus sum! I have been baptized!' precisely because it had been done *to* him, not *by* him.''[31]

While Luther insisted all along that justification by faith excluded the necessity of good works with regard to salvation, he nevertheless believed that good works would follow once a person was justified. In his lectures on Romans, Luther taught that the new people lived a life of righteousness, performing good works, but always as people who still lived in their sins. ''Thus when the apostle says that a man is justified from works of the law ... he is not speaking about the works which are performed in order that we may seek justification. Because these are no longer the works of the law but of grace and faith ...''[32] Luther explains that a baptized Christian may have sins. Nevertheless, they are not sins, since Christ covers them. In a sense Christians are sinful, yet they are not able to sin, because their sins are not held against them. In Luther's words: ''Then it only remains for us to stay in our sins and to cry [in hope] to God that He would deliver us from them .... For it is sufficient that our sin displeases us, even though we do not get entirely rid of it.''[33] Thus on the one hand, good works, according to Luther, are the result and evidence of justification, and on the other, the sins that remain and are still being committed by the justified sinner are not held against him because of faith in Christ's work of redemption. It appears that Luther's *sola fide* principle resulted in an emphasis on a judicial, that is legal, righteousness before God, rather than on a real, demonstrable, righteousness before men and in society. As Luther puts it: ''Our doctrine is pure because it is a gift of God. But in our life there still is something sinful and punishable. However, this is forgiven and not imputed. It is not put on the books against us; but *remissio peccatorum* (remission of sin) is placed over it, and the sin is wiped out.''[34]

The Anabaptists believed that Luther's doctrine of justification by faith alone led to loose morals among Lutherans. They agreed with the Reformer that man is saved by the grace of God, but they repudiated his idea of an enslaved will and maintained that a justified person had to perform good works to make good his salvation. This caused Luther to brand the Anabaptists as Romanists, that is, people who believed in "works righteousness." However, it was difficult for him to deny that there was a marked difference between the ethical life of the Anabaptists and that of his followers. Writing in 1527, Luther characterized the Anabaptists as follows: "The new sect of Anabaptists is making astonishing progress. They are people who conduct themselves with very great outward propriety, and go through fire and water without flinching in support of their doctrines."[35] However, for Luther the good life and steadfastness of the Anabaptists was a trick of the devil intended to lead Christians astray and to undermine his newly discovered gospel of the Reformation.

While Luther was not entirely indifferent to how his followers lived, it is nevertheless true that Luther's doctrine of justification led among his followers to a lack of concern for ethics and to an indifference with regard to "good works". In 1522 the Bohemian Brethren were much interested in the Lutheran reformation, but they found fault with the discipline and moral life among Lutherans. When they complained to Luther about this, the Reformer was annoyed but promised to correct the moral laxity among his followers.[36] Staupitz too, Luther's former superior in the monastery, advised Luther not to disregard the moral aspect of the gospel, stating that he saw many persons who abused the gospel for the freedom of the flesh.[37] Similarly the German poet Hans Sachs, a contemporary and strong supporter of Luther, addressed the Lutherans as follows: "There is much cry and little wool about you. If you have no use for brotherly love, you are no disciples of Christ. If you were really evangelical as you profess to be, you would lead a godly life like the Apostles."[38] Philip Melanchthon pointed out in 1525 that "the common people adhered to Luther only because they think that no further religious duty will be laid upon them."[39] The bigamy of Philip of Hesse, one of the most prominent Lutheran princes, and Luther's embarrassing involvement in the case, are well known and need not be retold here.[40]

Luther criticized his followers for not living according to the Gospel. In 1530 he blamed his "lazy and indifferent" ministers for the people's disregard for the sacraments and the Christian life. The longer we preach the gospel, he lamented, the deeper the people plunge into greed, pride and luxury.[41] Luther's doctrine of justification by faith was often abused by those who had no desire to follow the Christian principles of living. As one Evangelical minister stated: Justification by faith was made to cover all sins; hence one could often see the justified and the old man side by side, with the old man not a bit changed.[42]

II. The Anabaptists on Justification

The Anabaptists were not slow to detect the contradiction between the Luther profession of faith and the ethical disregard among the followers of the Reformer. For the Anabaptists and for the later Mennonites, Luther's *sola fide* doctrine was not only an overemphasis of a biblical truth but a heretical teaching which led to un-Christian consequences. Writing in 1541 on the "Faith of the Lutherans," Menno Simons states:

"The Lutherans teach and believe that faith alone saves, without any assistance by works. They emphasize this doctrine so as to make it appear as though works were not even necessary; yes, that faith is of such a nature that it cannot tolerate any work alongside of it. And therefore the important and earnest epistle of James (because he reproved such a frivolous, vain doctrine and faith) is esteemed and treated as a 'strawy epistle'. What bold folly! ... Let everyone take heed how he teaches. For with this same doctrine they [the Lutherans] have led the reckless and ignorant people, great and small, city dweller and cottager alike, into such a fruitless, unregenerate life, and have given them such a free rein, that one would scarcely find such an ungodly and abominable life among Turks and Tartars as among these people. Their open deeds bear testimony for the abundant eating and drinking; the excessive pomp and splendor; the fornicating, lying, cheating, cursing; the swearing by the wounds of the Lord ...; the shedding of blood, the fighting, etc., which are found among many of them have neither measure nor bounds."

Lest some people might think that he is exaggerating, Menno adds: "What I know I write, and what I have heard and seen I testify, and I know that I testify the truth."[43]

From its very beginning in 1525 Anabaptism taught that justification by faith and works of love must go hand in hand. Regeneration and sanctification cannot be separated. Balthasar Hubmaier, writing in 1526, stated that "faith alone and by itself is not sufficient for salvation ... I confess this article with all my strength: that faith by itself alone is not worthy to be called faith, for there can be no true faith without the works of love."[44] Hans Denck, the apostle of love among the Anabaptists, wrote similarly: "Faith is the obedience to God and the confidence in his promise through Jesus Christ."[45] Michael Sattler, one of the prime movers in the Schleitheim conference of 1527, wrote: "... when one speaks of justification through Christ, one must also speak of that faith which cannot be without works of repentance ... [and] love ... when one speaks of works, one must preach not ... the works of law but the works of faith."[46] According to Sattler, a believer's "works" are not his own works but works of God performed by faith.[47] Sattler advocates a "middle path" with regard to faith and works. Referring to the mainline Reformers, Sattler says that the "scribes" turn aside "to the right, and teach in the manner of 'gospel' a faith without works, and take the poor obedient Christ ... as their satisfaction, but will not hear when he says [in] Lk.9: 'come, follow me'."[48]

Melchior Hoffman, who had a great influence on the Dutch and North German Anabaptists in general and on Menno Simons in particular, believed that "faith cannot make one justified," if there are no fruits of faith.[49] Rhetorically and by way of an example Hoffman asks: "For what kind of faith would that be in the case of a woman with her husband, to whom she publicly adhered and confessed to be her lord and bridegroom, and nevertheless continuously went out to commit adultery and illicit love-making with others?"[50]

Pilgram Marpeck, writing in his *Confession of 1532*, also combines faith and the fruit of faith. He speaks of the "true assurance of God in Christ," which is faith, and of being made alive in the spirit to perform works of righteousness such as "joy, comfort, confidence, and true love, with a clean heart and sincere faith, with patience, meakness and lowliness of heart, with mercy and peacemaking, friendliness and true godliness."[51] In this quotation we have in a sense the Anabaptists' confession of faith.

Jacob Hutter, after whom the Hutterites are named, in 1535 answered those who charged that the Anabaptists boast about their good works and claim to be sinless:

"... we can take no credit for good as natural men, but we give all glory and praise to God to whom it rightfully belongs. For it is obvious that man in himself cannot think anything good, let alone do it, as Paul says. For because of the grace of God we know that the works which we do and carry out as men count for nothing before God on that day. Inasmuch, however, as God does them in us through his grace and his spirit by whom all the believers are governed, they are good, just, pleasing and acceptable to God."[52]

Peter Riedeman, also an early leader of the Hutterites, wrote in 1542:

"Faith is not the empty illusion that those men think who only bear it about with them in their mouths, and know no more about it; who think that Christianity is in words only, and therefore hold and regard each and all as Christians, no matter how they live, if they but confess Christ with their mouths.

True and well-founded faith, however, is not of men but a gift of God, and is given only to those who fear God."[53]

Dirk Philips, a co-worker of Menno Simons, wrote in 1556 that while regeneration is the work of God in man, there is an element of cooperation between the Holy Spirit and the obedience of the individual believer.[54] Regeneration and obedience to Christ, according to Dirk Philips, are two sides of the same process. As he put it:

"But this is the beginning and the end of the teaching of Jesus Christ ... that we sincerely repent, believe the gospel, are baptized upon our faith in the name of the Holy Trinity ... and are diligent by the grace of Gopd to observe all that Christ has commanded us."[55]

Coming back to the organizer of the Mennonite movement, Menno Simons acknowledges his debt to Martin Luther, mentioning especially the help he received from the German Reformer in his spiritual struggles prior to leaving the priesthood and joining Anabaptism. Menno Simons accepted Luther's *sola fide* but saw it as one side only of the Christian experience. Writing concerning ''Justification'' in his *Christian Foundation* book, Menno Simons explains:

"You see, kind reader, we do not seek our salvation in works, words, or sacraments as do the learned ones, although they accuse us of that very thing, but we seek them only in Christ Jesus and in no other means in heaven or on earth .... But that we abhor carnal works and desire to conform ourselves to His Word and commandment, according to our weakness, we do because He so taught and commanded us. For whosoever does not walk according to this doctrine, proves in fact that he does not believe on Him or know Him and that he is not in the communion of the saints.''[56]

From this lengthy quotation and those of the other Anabaptist leaders it becomes fairly evident that the Anabaptist view of justification was not merely a slight shift in emphasis from Luther's position but a basic difference in understanding scriptures on this point. For the Anabaptists both scriptures and their experience required that faith and discipleship belong together and cannot be separated.

There is irony in the Anabaptists' opposition to Luther and his basic theological position. Alfred Coutts writes: ''Just as Luther had traced all the moral chaos of his time to the [theological] errors of Rome, so the spiritual reformers [including the Anabaptists] found the explanation of the moral and spiritual degeneration of the Reformation age in the doctrinal errors of the Reformed Church.''[57] Luther for his part, however, felt that the criticism of the Anabaptists was an indication that they lacked the Holy Spirit, for the Spirit, according to Luther, condemns false doctrines only and is infinitely patient with those who are ''weak in the faith.''[58] In a sermon in 1533 Luther warned his congregation against the apparent godly life of the Anabaptists. The Anabaptists, according to Luther, are like wolves in sheep's clothing; they do not curse, they pray and read the Word of God, they are patient in suffering and not vengeful against their enemies, and to all appearances live like good Christians. All this is good and worthy of emulation, but one must be on guard against thinking that their outward piety is proof that their theology is correct.[59]

There is another irony with regard to the relationship between Luther and the Anabaptist's attempt to live as justified Christians.

It was particularly the young Luther who had not only influenced the Anabaptists in their faith and theology but had actually caused many of them to leave the Roman Catholic Church. Now that the Anabaptists were trying to live according to the Reformer's teachings, they were criticized and persecuted by their spiritual father. There is a tone of reproach and sadness in the following excerpt from a Swiss Brethren document, directed against all mainline reformers:

"The ministers of the established church at first have taught this evangelical doctrine, and some of them teach it even today, that one should abstain from sin, lead a pious, irreproachable Christian life, be born of God and regenerated, manifest Christian love, follow Christ, bear the cross .... And now, when we by God's grace desire to do, believe, teach, and live, in accord with their first teaching, we are to them an abomination, they cannot tolerate us, they defame and reproach us in this our Christian faith ... as if it were heretical and erroneous."[60]

To suggest that Luther deliberately misunderstood and misrepresented the motives and life of the Anabaptists either to justify the often loose living of his followers or to warn people against what he considered to be their errors, is to misunderstand the Reformer and what was involved. Luther was not altogether indifferent to the question of ethics among his followers. He had preached and written concerning the necessity of "good works" in the life of those who claimed to have experienced the grace of God, and he had to agree that in the realm of morals and discipleship the Anabaptists often put the Lutherans to shame. For example, when Caspar Schwenckfeld, the Silesian nobleman and reformer, spoke to Luther in 1525 about the onesidedness of justification by faith and that this led to a lax ethical life among his followers, Luther agreed. "Yes, dear Caspar," Luther said, "true Christians are not as yet all too common. I would like to see two together."[61] However, just as Luther in his break with Rome was not primarily concerned with the alleged lack of ethics among Catholics, so also was he not overly impressed with the pious living of the Anabaptists. He knew of course that what a person believed often led to a corresponding conduct; but he also believed, rightly or wrongly, that right conduct was not necessarily a sign of correct doctrine. And right dogma mattered more to Luther than right living, as we have seen. Thus when he examined the beliefs and theological emphases of the Anabaptists and found that they contradicted his understanding and experience of the Word of God on the most vital point in his theology, he did not doubt for a moment that the Anabaptists were wrong and that he was right. Luther feared that as soon as the human element received priority in the life of a Christian—and in Anabaptism he believed that it did—it would lead to human pride and to a minimizing of God's work in the life of individuals. Man, according to Luther, is saved and sustained by the grace of God; good works must be the result of God's grace and an expression of gratitude for what God has done in Christ. That his *sola fide* often led to a disregard of discipline among his followers and that his view of the enslaved will was sometimes used as a pretext for carnal living, the Reformer recognized and lamented. On balance, however, Luther decided to retain what he had come to believe about the grace of God and considered the ethical life among his followers as less important than his doctrine of *sola fide*.

Thus the two Reformation movements, Lutheranism and Anabaptism, with their differing ideological foci, were consciously in opposition to each other. Harold S. Bender points out correctly: "Lutheranism saw in Anabaptist discipleship a work-righteousness and legalism, while Anabaptism saw in Luther's 'faith only'-justification a lifeless faith and compromise with the claims and call of Christ."[62] Bender, however, adds less convincingly: "The two positions, purified of extremes and misunderstandings, are not in necessary conflict, but should be complimentary parts of a full New Testament Christianity."[63] Luther and the Anabaptists, it seems to me, understood each others positions quite well. In their understanding of faith and life they were diametrically opposed to each other.

It is perhaps too much to expect that the gap between the two positions could have been bridged in the 16th century. Compromise, conciliation and tolerance were not priorities among the various reformation groups. Had there been a reconciliation between the two positions and groups, one wonders which side would have given up more in the interest of unity and concord. Of interest and significance is that when Bonhoeffer sought to bridge the gap between justification by faith and discipleship, he moved beyond Luther and came close to the Anabaptist position.

III. Bonhoeffer on Justification

In the 1930s Dietrich Bonhoeffer wrote his now famous book *The Cost of Discipleship* which was to make the concepts of "cheap" and "costly grace" household words in theological circles. But it was not until after World War II that the Protestant world experienced the impact of Bonhoeffer's life, thought and martyrdom. Not only Lutherans felt the influence of Bonhoeffer's thinking but also Mennonites were drawn to the life and teaching of this most noble person and theologian. I recall how Mennonite ministers and teachers quoted Bonhoeffer in their sermons and writings with approval and almost equated his *The Cost of Discipleship* with the "Sermon on the Mount" itself. The only flaw which Mennonites found in Bonhoeffer, was his painful decision to give up his earlier pacifism in favor of active resistance and political involvement.[64] But even this "failure" on the part of Bonhoeffer was seen in the light of circumstances and forgiven because the theology and ethics of this theologian were Anabaptist-Mennonite throughout.

A mere glance at the Table of Contents of *The Cost of Discipleship* is needed to indicate that the subject matter of the book is "Mennonite." Such headings as "Discipleship and the Cross," "The Visible Community," "The Brother," "Revenge," "The Enemy," "The Simplicity of the Carefree Life," "The Separation of the Disciple Community"-to name only a few-are concepts which were most familiar to Anabaptist-Mennonites from the beginning of their history. In our consideration of *The Cost of Discipleship,* we shall deal with Chapter One only, the chapter in which Bonhoeffer discusses Luther's concepts of grace and faith.

According to Bonhoeffer, Lutherans have misunderstood the Reformer on the question of justification. For Luther, Bonhoeffer argues, it was the *justification of the sinner* that was at issue, but his followers saw in Luther's doctrine a justification *for* sin.

For Luther the grace of God was costly, but among his followers grace had become cheap:

"...the outcome of the Reformation was the victory, not of Luther's perception of grace in all its purity and costliness, but of the vigilant religious instinct of man for the place where grace is to be obtained at the cheapest price. All that was needed was a subtle and almost imperceptible change of emphasis, and the damage was done."[65]

Bonhoeffer believed that Luther saw faith and works of love together whereas his followers separated faith and discipleship. As Bonhoeffer puts it:

"When he spoke of grace, Luther always implied as a corollary that it cost him his own life, the life which was now for the first time subjected to the absolute obedience of Christ....Luther had said that grace alone can save; his followers took up his doctrine and repeated it word for word. But they left out its invariable corollary, the obligation of discipleship."[66]

It is of course true that for Luther—certainly for the young Luther—the grace of God was costly and that he had embarked upon life of true discipleship. But whether Luther had taught the cost of discipleship "in all its purity" or whether his teaching was "imperceptibly changed" is very much an open question. What is more, when Bonhoeffer in his defense of Luther states that "there was no need for Luther always to mention that corollary explicitly, for he always spoke as one who had been led by grace to the strictest following of Christ,"[67] Bonhoeffer leaves himself open for serious questions. Did Luther as a student of scriptures and human nature not know the tendency of the human heart? Did not his friends and opponents point out to him the one-sidedness of his doctrine and the results of justification by faith alone? And did not Luther inspite of this adhere to his doctrine and its emphasis in all his writings? True, Luther did not deny the necessity of good works in the lives of his followers, but he always taught that works "are not good in themselves, but must be done in faith and in the assurance of God's favor"68 and that they would follow once a person was justified.

Bonhoeffer believed, as did the Anabaptists, that the Lutherans had destroyed the Reformation. Pointing out the irony and paradox of the Lutheran reformation, Bonhoeffer states: "Judged by the standard of Luther's doctrine, that of his followers was unassailable, and yet their orthodoxy spelt the end and destruction of the Reformation as the revelation on earth of the costly grace of God."[69] Bonhoeffer becomes most sarcastic when he adds:

"To be 'Lutheran' must mean that we leave the following of Christ to Nomians, Calvinists and Anabaptists—and all this for the sake of grace. We justified the world, and condemned as heretics those who tried to follow Christ. The result was that a nation became Christian and Lutheran, but at the cost of true discipleship."[70]

In his defense of Luther and in his criticism of Lutherans, Bonhoeffer seems to be ill at ease with regard to Luther's apparently flippant pronouncements about human weakness. Bonhoeffer thus interprets Luther's *Pecca fortiter* ("Sin boldly") as meaning that this must be understood as a principle of sin which is in opposition to the principle of grace. It is not that Luther advocated that Christians sin boldly, but that when sin beset them they should have courage to believe that while sin was great and Christians are and remain sinners, the grace of God is greater still to forgive their sins. Bonhoeffer adds:

"For Luther 'Sin boldly' could only be his very last refuge, the consolation for one whose attempts to follow Christ had taught him that he can never become sinless, who in his fear of sin despairs of the grace of God."[71]

Bonhoeffer concludes his interpretation of Luther's justification by confessing that "although our church is orthodox as far as her doctrine of grace is concerned, we are no longer sure that we are members of a Church which follows its Lord."[72] Bonhoeffer believes that as Lutherans they must "attemp to recover a true understanding of the mutual relationship between grace and discipleship."[73]

With regard to Bonhoeffer's interpretation of Luther's *sola fide* we might ask with Eberhard Bethge, Bonhoeffer's friend and biographer, whether Bonhoeffer had not betrayed the Lutheran Reformation by developing a new doctrine of sanctification.[74] Bonhoeffer himself wrote to Bethge, suggesting that his book *The Cost of Discipleship* was a dangerous book.[75] What he no doubt meant was, as John D. Godsey suggests: "the danger...was not one of 'works righteousness', that is, that we would try to justify ourselves before God by doing good works. Rather, it was that our efforts to lead a holy life of discipleship might lead us to be more interested in ourselves than in others. We might want to make something out of ourselves rather than 'being there for others'."[76] Moreover, Bonhoeffer believed that justification by faith "needs re-installation by the preservation of the costliness of the gift."[77]

In all his later writings, Bonhoeffer continued to see grace and discipleship as necessary twins in a Christian's life. As a Lutheran he continued to cling to the Reformation principle of *sola fide*, but he modified or expanded this principle to include ethics and "works." The following quotation from his *Ethics* is not only representative of Bonhoeffer's concern but also an apt summary of what Anabaptists themselves believed with regard to justification and ethics:

"...a justified life, a life justified by grace alone...yet not by grace alone, but also by faith alone. That is the teaching of the Bible and of the Reformation. A life is not justified by love or by hope, but only by faith. For indeed faith alone sets life upon a new foundation, and it is this new foundation alone that justifies my being able to live before God. This foundation is the life, the death and the resurrection of the Lord Jesus Christ...But faith never is alone. As surely as faith is the true presence of Christ, so surely too, is it accompanied by love and hope. It would be a false faith, a dissembling faith, a hypocritical and self-invented faith such as can never justify, if it were not accompanied by love and hope. It would be a vain repetition of articles of faith, a dead faith, if it were not accompanied by the works of penitence and love."[78]

Regin Prenter argues that Bonhoeffer and the young Luther were theologically most similar. In both there is an attempt to correlate "the theology of the cross with the theology of the Word."[79] Similarly James W. Woelfel points out that throughout his writings Bonhoeffer like Luther "urgently calls the church and the Christian to take the risk of decisive words and actions on behalf of God's world."[80] And again Woelfel writes: "Justification by faith alone meant for Bonhoeffer, as for Luther, liberation for courageous and responsible speaking and acting in the World."[81]

This interpretation of Bonhoeffer is no doubt correct as far as it goes, but specifically on the question of faith versus works, Bonhoeffer, while claiming Luther for his view, actually moves beyond the Reformer. As Eberhard Bethge puts it: "In addition to scriptural sources Bonhoeffer tries hard to find hints for this view in the Lutheran Confession. But he found only hints....He actually was ploughing new ground or at least ploughing in another climate."[82] In an Anabaptist climate? one might ask. Similarly William Kuhns observes correctly concerning Bonhoeffer's *The Cost of Discipleship:* "For the first time Bonhoeffer clarifies doctrinally his relationship with Luther and reveals a fresh point of view not inherent in Luther's works."[83] Moreover, in his appeal to the visible church community, in his emphasis on the necessity of good works, and in his numerous references to the cross in the life of Christians, Bonhoeffer "has taken up new lines of questioning, which eventually would lead him further from Luther."[84] For Bonhoeffer, then, justification is God's process of making the believer just, and nothing else; "a doctrine of justification as a mere forensic process," as Hans Pfeifer points out, "is impossible from his [Bonhoeffer's] point of view."[85]

IV. Conclusion

The grace-works debate will no doubt continue after the 500th anniversary celebrations have come to an end. Yet while Catholics and those of the Radical Reformation tradition will continue to view with theological misgivings what they consider to be Luther's one-sided position of faith only, they will no doubt acknowledge the contribution the Reformer has made in the recovery of a Christian understanding of the grace of God through faith. No one else has apporached the clarity with which Luther discussed works and grace. His total dependence for salvation on God's grace, through faith, was the great foundation-laying message for Christian discipleship.[86] In a sense Luther's foundation had to come first before the Anabaptists could begin to erect their structure of discipleship and ethics.[87]

It must be stressed, however, that the difference between Luther and the Anabaptists on faith and discipleship was not merely one of emphasis but a difference in fundamentals, which was recognized by both sides. In Luther the Christian faith and life depended wholly on God and his sovereign work of regeneration. All human efforts and works were excluded; good works were merely the results of faith. For the Anabaptists, on the other hand, God through the Holy Spirit appealed to the human will to believe, to accept God's forgiveness, and to do the will of God in following Christ. Faith and works of righteousness were integral parts of a person's faith and life. To work out one's salvation with fear and trembling was part of this theology. In Luther regeneration and sanctification were separated theologically and in time. In Anabaptism the two were one and the same process; there could not be one without the other.

There were of course many factors which had led Luther to his theological position and his inability (or unwillingness) to yield to the Anabaptists' view of justification: his background and struggles in the monastery; his view of man and human sinfulness; his life-long agonizing over justification and questions with regard to faith and certainty in his own life;[88] and his personality which would not yield once his mind was made up, no matter what or who the opposition.

The tragedy in the struggle between the Lutheran and the Anabaptist positions is a chapter in itself. Not only did the two positions prevent Lutherans and Anabaptists from uniting in a common cause, but they also led to Lutheran determination to persecute and silence Anabaptism. For Anabaptists the readiness of Lutherans to persecute those who dissented from orthodoxy was further evidence that the theological position of Luther and his followers was un-Christian. Moreover, Luther's many inflamatory writings and actions against the peasants, the Anabaptists, and the Jews certainly did not reassure those who already had grave doubts about the Reformer and his theology.

That a Lutheran theologian of our time should stress those aspects of the Christian faith and life for which the Anabaptists lived and died 450 years ago, is not only ironic but almost comic. For Anabaptist-Mennonites it is a case of God's mills grinding slowly, yet grinding exceedingly small. Bonhoeffer's *re*interpretation of Luther and his Christian existentialism—that is, his application of the gospel to society—is what the Anabaptists and Mennonites have believed and tried to practise with varying degrees of success and failure all along. Thus on the 500th anniversary of Luther's birth we can not only speak of *Luther's* significance for the church today, but also of the contributions of Anabaptism to the Church and society. Add to this the seriousness with which individuals in the Church and society discuss today such issues as peace, nonviolence, brotherhood and community, discipleship and civil disobedience—all 16th century Anabaptist principles and practices—and the divine comedy is complete. The 16th century Anabaptists have been vindicated.

On May 4th of this year (1983) Werner Lech, bishop of Thuringia, publicly expressed regret concerning Luther's and his adherents' sins against the Anabaptists. In his words: "Our thankfulness for the legacy of Martin Luther is linked with a plea for forgiveness from all against whom our fathers in the heat of the Reformation sinned."[89] This symposium is also a most remarkable achievement. Lutherans, Catholics, Reformed, and Mennonites have come together to dialogue and fellowship with each other. It is not indifference in matters of faith and morals which has brought us together, but the memory of one of the greatest Reformation figures whose teaching has influenced the entire Christian church and western civilization. This symposium is also an expression of our belief that what our broken world needs is the grace of God through faith as expressed in Christian discipleship.

ENDNOTES

The author is grateful for a D A A D (German Academic Exchange Service) grant, which enabled him to work on this paper during the summer of 1983.

1. Dietrich Bonhoeffer, *Letters and Papers from Prison*, The Enlarged Edition, ed. by Eberhard Bethge (New York: Macmillan Publ. Co., Inc., 1971), p. 123.

2. Ibid., p. 123.

3. Ibid., p. 123.

4. James W. Woelfel, *Bonhoeffer's Theology: Classical and Revolutionary* (New York: Abingdon Press, 1970), pp. 313-314.

5. Heinrich Boehmer, *Martin Luther: Road to Reformation*, trans. by J.W. Doberstein and T.G. Tappert (New York: Living Age Books, 1957), p. 87.

6. WA 40,I:137; LW 26:70.

7. WA 47:275.

8. See Heiko A. Oberman, "'Iustitia Christi' and 'Iustitia Dei': Luther and the Scholastic Doctrines of Justification," *Harvard Theological Review* 59,1 (January, 1966):1-26.

9. WA 10,II:262. It has been shown that "Luther from the very beginning demonstrated an astonishing degree of independence from his teachers, whether Staupitz or the books, and that his theology was far more than the sum of the parts of his theological heritage." Lewis W. Spitz, *Renaissance Quarterly* 34,4 (Winter, 1981):577, in a review of David C. Steinmetz, *Luther and Staupitz: An Essay in the Intellectual Origins of the Reformation*, 1980.

10. WA Br 3:643.

11. WA Br 5:531.

12. WA 25:375.

13. WA 40,I:48; LW 26:9.

14. WA 10,III:18-19; LW 51:77. See Mark U. Edwards, Jr., *Luther and the False Brethren* (Stanford, Calif.: Stanford Univ. Press, 1975), p. 29.

15. Quoted by Jaroslav Pelikan, *Spirit Versus Structure: Luther and the Institutions of*

the Church (New York, Evanston, London: Harper and Row, 1968), p. 134. See also Thomas M. McDonough, *The Law and the Gospel in Luther: A Study of Martin Luther's Confessional Writings* (London: Oxford University Press, 1963).

16. WA DB 6:10:33-34.

17. WA DB 7:384-387; LW 35:396.

18. Hans H. W. Kramm, *The Theology of Martin Luther* (London: J. Clarke), p. 121.

19. WA 7:42-49; LW 31:334-343.

20. WA 7:278-279; LW 39:121-135.

21. WA TR 1:294:19-22, nr. 624; LW 54:110.

22. WA 56: 263-267; LW 25:251-254.

23. WA 1:355-364; LW 31:42-55.

24. WA 2:146:29-32; LW 31:299-300.

25. LW 44:17-18.

26. WA 6:229:17-18; LW 44:54.

27. Heinrich Bornkamm, *Luther's World of Thought*, trans. by M.H. Bertram (St. Louis: Concordia Publ. House, 1958), p. 112.

28. Harry Loewen, *Luther and the Radicals* (Waterloo: Wilfrid Laurier University Press, 1974), p. 43.

29. WA 26:144-174; LW 40:229-262.

30. The Anabaptists were not slow to detect a contradiction in Luther's emphasis on justifying faith and his argument in favour of "dormant faith" in infants and the validity of infant baptism. As Menno Simons wrote in his *Foundation of Christian Doctrine* (1539): "If Luther writes this as his sincere opinion [about the faith of infants], then he proves that he has written in vain a great deal concerning faith and its power. But if he writes this to please men, may God have mercy on him." Menno Simons, *The Complete Writings*, trans. from the Dutch by Leonard Verduin and ed. by John C. Wenger, with a biography by H.S. Bender (Scottdale: Herald Press, 1956), p. 126.

31. Pelikan, p. 96.

32. LW 25:251-252.

33. Ibid., p. 254.

34. WA 33:371:32-41; LW 23:198-306.

35. Quoted by Alfred Coutts, *Hans Denck (1495-1527): Humanist and Heretic* (Edinburgh: Macniven & Wallace, 1927), p. 114.

36. Edward Langton, *History of the Moravian Church: The Story of the First International Protestant Church* (London: Allen & Unwin, 1956), pp. 41-43.

37. See David C. Steinmetz, *Luther and Staupitz: An Essay in the Intellectual Origins of the Protestant Reformation* (Durham: Duke University Press, 1980).

38. Quoted by A. Coutts, op. cit., p. 244.

39. John Horsch, *Mennonites in Europe,* 2nd ed. (Scottdale: Mennonite Publ. House, 1950), p. 28.

40. See Luther's letters concerning this affair in Preserved Smith, *The Life and Letters of Martin Luther* (London: John Murray, 1911), pp. 373-386.

41. Cf. Dr. Martin Luther's *Saemmtliche Werke* (Erlangen: Carl Heyder, 1832), 23:166-167; WA 30,II:598:1-4; LW 38:100.

42. See Philip Schaff, *History of the Christian Church,* rpr. of 2nd ed., revised (Grand Rapids: Wm. B. Eerdmans, 1953), 7:667.

43. Menno Simons, p. 333. Menno Simons had his own theological obsession, which may not be all that unrelated to the subject of this paper. I am referring to Menno Simon's emphasis on the "pure church," the church of Christ "without spot or wrinkle," as Menno called the church time and again. This emphasis led to both thological and ethical consequences which already in Menno's time were an embarrassment to Mennonites.
Following a long tradition, begun by the Valentinians at the time of Tertullian and continued by Caspar Schwenckfeld and Melchior Hoffman in the 16th century, Menno Simons held a peculiar view with regard to the incarnation of Christ, a view closely related to his concept of a pure church. Christ, in becoming man had merely passed through Mary his mother, thus remaining fully divine and becoming less than human. Christ's body was according to this view "heavenly flesh," not human, for whatever is human is of necessity tainted by sin. And since Christ is the Head of a "pure Church," Menno argued, Christ himself must be the pure and holy one.
This emphasis on the "pure church" led to high expectations and standards in the realm of ethics among Mennonites, a harsh application of the ban and shunning, and it resulted in a fair amount of legalism throughout Mennonite history.

44. Walter Klaassen: ed., *Anabaptism in Outline: Selected Primary Sources* (Kitchener and Scottdale: Herald Press, 1981), p. 44.

45. Ibid., p. 46.

46. Ibid., pp. 56-57.

47. Ibid., p. 57.

48. Ibid., p. 57.

49. Ibid., p. 58.

50. Ibid., p. 58.

51. Ibid., pp. 145-146.

52. Ibid., p. 60.

53. Ibid., p. 63.

54. The idea of cooperation between the individual and God in man's salvation was especially suspect for Luther.

55. Klaassen, pp. 68-69.

56. Menno Simons, pp. 504-505.

57. Coutts, p. 81

58. Dr. Martin Luther's *Saemmtlich Werke* (Frankfurt A. M. and Erlangen: Verlag von Heyder and Zimmer, 1853), 53:263-265.

59. WA 26:161-163; LW 40:248-250.

60. Quoted by John Horsch, ''The Character of the Evangelical Anabaptists as Reported by Contemporary Reformation Writers,'' *Mennonite Quarterly Review* 8 (July, 1934):129.

61. *Corpus Schwenkfeldianorum* (Leipzig: Breitkopf & Haertel, 1911), 2:281:4-5. In this Luther predated Friedrich Nietzsche by three and a half centuries. According to Nietzsche, the one Christian that had existed died on the cross!

62. *The Mennonite Encyclopedia: A Comprehensive Reference Work on the Anabaptist-Mennonite Movement* (Scottdale: Mennonite Publ. House, 1959) 4:1076.

63. Ibid., 4:1076.

64. On Bonhoeffer's change from pacifism to resistance, see William Kuhns, *In Pursuit of Dietrich Bonhoeffer* (London: Burns and Oates, 1967), pp. 221-232.

65. Dietrich Bonhoeffer, *The Cost of Discipleship,* trans. by R.H. Fuller (London: S C M Press, 1948). p. 43.

66. Ibid., p. 43.

67. Ibid., p. 43.

68. Cf. above ftn. 25 and 26.

69. Bonhoeffer, *The Cost of Discipleship,* pp. 43-44.

70. Ibid., p. 47

71. Ibid., p. 46. There were other statements in Luther's works about which Bonhoeffer no doubt felt the need for careful interpretation. For example, in one of his Table Talks of 1532 Luther is reported as saying: "Christ was an adulterer for the first time with the woman at the well, for it was said, 'nobody knows what he's doing with her.' Again with Magdalene, and still again with the adulterous woman in John 8, whom he let off so easily. So the good Christ had to become an adulterer before he died." WA TR 2:107:21-25, nr. 1472; LW 54:154. Such statements, and possibly others, Bonhoeffer had in mind when he wrote in his *Christology:* "Luther says the [Christ] is himself robber, murderer and adulterer as we are, for he bears our sins, and in so doing describes the ultimate foundation of all Christological statements. As the one who bears our sins, and no one else, he is sinless, holy eternal, the Lord, the Son of the Father." *Christology,* introd. by Edwin H. Robertson, trans. by John Bowden (London: Collins, 1971), p. 113. It might be added that for Anabaptist-Mennonites Luther's statement about Jesus's adultery would have been blasphemous.

72. Bonhoeffer, *The Cost of Discipleship,* p. 49.

73. Ibid., p. 49.

74. See Ronald Gregor Smith, ed., *World Come of Age* (Philadelphia: Fortress Press, 1967), p. 57.

75. John D. Godsey, "The Legacy of Dietrich Bonhoeffer," p. 165 in A.J. Klassen, ed., *A Bonhoeffer Legacy: Essays in Understanding* (Grand Rapids: Wm. B. Eerdmans, 1981).

76. Ibid., p. 165.

77. Smith, p. 57. Benjamin A. Reist is correct when he states: "For Bonhoeffer...faith exists only as obedience....There is a hidden depth [in Bonhoeffer's] contention that faith does not hold chronological priority over obedience." *The Promise of Bonhoeffer* (Philadelphia and New York: J.B. Lippincott, 1969), p. 58. See also Dallas M. Roark, *Dietrich Bonhoeffer* (Waco: Word Books, 1972), pp. 75-80.

78. Dietrich Bonhoeffer, *Ethics,* ed. by Eberhard Bethge (New York: Macmillan, 1965), pp. 121-122.

79. Smith, pp. 180-181.

80. Woelfel, p. 79.

81. Ibid., p. 170.

82. Smith, pp. 57-58.

83. Kuhns, p. 86.

84. Ibid., p. 88.

85. Hans Pfeifer, "The Forms of Justification: On the question of the Structure in Dietrich Bonhoeffer's Theology," in *A Bonhoeffer Legacy*, p. 32.

86. Abraham P. Toews, *The Problem of Mennonite Ethics* (Grand Rapids: Wm. B. Eerdmans, 1963), p. 125.

87. Ibid., p. 125.

88. Roland H. Bainton, "Luther's Struggle for Faith," in Lewis W. Spitz, ed., *The Reformation: Basic Interpretations* (Lexington, Toronto, London: D.C. Heath, 1972), pp. 200-212.

89. Bill Yoder, "East German Lutherans request forgiveness from Anabaptists," *Mennonite Reporter*, May 16, 1983.

IV THE RELATIONSHIP BETWEEN LUTHER AND THE LUTHERAN CONFESSIONS
by
Lowell C. Green

The quinquecentennial observances of the birth of Martin Luther in 1983 brought forth outstanding studies from Luther scholars out of the Roman Catholic, Reformed, and Free Church traditions. Many Lutherans were surprised to see fine Luther research coming out of other confessions at a time when they themselves were neglecting their reformer. If the anniversary has produced anything in the true spirit of Luther, it will have brought Christians today back to the Gospel which he rediscovered. Lutheran theology today stands in a crisis while it fluctuates between its tradition and the contemporary scene. It is to be hoped that the quincentenary will have illuminated both past and present.

Theologians in the Lutheran churches today need to reconstruct their theology. There are four resources: The Bible, the works of Luther, the Lutheran Confessions, and human experience, including contemporary society. We must leave for another occasion the relationship between Tradition and Scripture, or between History and Contemporary Thinking. Our task instead is to deal with another problem: **The Relationship Between Luther and the Lutheran Confessions.** To what extent do these two resources agree and where do they differ? Many European Lutherans make the difference very great, they regard Luther as the authoritative voice in the church, and they downplay the Confessions. In North America, the opposite trend is common: The Confessions take an almost legalistic position and Luther is downgraded. Luther is no longer a "teacher in the church."

Writers of the Lutheran Confessions saw no discrepancy and no possibility of having one without the other. After all, Luther had written three of the seven Symbols, and the Formula of Concord virtually canonized his writings. It called him "that precious man of God, Dr. Luther."[1] It spoke of his teachings as "the doctrine which the Blessed Dr. Luther drew out of God's Word and sturdily established against the papacy and other sects."[2] It declared him the chief teacher in the Lutheran Church[3] and it called his writings the standard for interpreting the Augsburg Confession.[4] It cited his *The Bondage of the Will* and *Lectures on Genesis* as standards of sound doctrine that were in accord with the Lutheran Confessions.[5] To reject Luther is to distance oneself from the Lutheran *Book of Concord* as well.

And still, much modern research holds that there are major discrepancies between the official Confessions of the Lutheran Church and the teachings of the great teacher. Probably the majority of Luther scholars reject parts of the Confessions and put forth interpretations of Luther that seem contradictory. Since the Lutheran churches accept these Symbols and require their subscription of pastors, congregations, and teachers, we are faced with a problem of major proportions. It is this problem that the present essay will seek to address. Our task will require familiarity with both Luther and the Confessions, and we shall have to consult them in the original languages. We shall attempt to see where the discrepancies between these two resources are real as well as where there is mutual agreement.

I. A Hermeneutics of Research

Hermeneutics is the science of interpretation. Many studies have been undertaken in Luther and the Confessions without due regard for sound hermeneutical procedures. Let us therefore consider some methods of interpretation which will help us to come to valid results.[6]

Lower criticism, that is, the critical study of the texts, is a necessary preparation. The works of Luther fall into five textual categories, which we shall quickly list in the descending order of reliability. Most reliable are those works, comparatively few in number, for which we have the original texts in Luther's handwriting. Second to these are the works which Luther himself edited for publication, where we no longer have autographs, but the printed texts appear faithfully to reproduce what we think he originally wrote. Third come the works which go back to lectures, sermons, or other oral deliveries, where the scribes were fully reliable; the best of these are the texts for which we have the original copybooks of Georg Roerer. Fourth come the works which others edited in cases where there are no longer any autographs of the amenuenses, instances were Luther may or may not have known or approved what was written or published. Last in reliability are the works for which there is little or no textual or editorial evidence, a category in which the *Table Talk* are an important part. It is commonly thought that these conversations of Luther have only a deutero-canonical authority, and that a conclusion about Luther may not be built solely upon *Table Talk* without corroboration from a more dependable source; however, it must also be borne in mind that many of the *Table Talks*, upon careful investigation, are relatively reliable. Nevertheless, the general rule that they must be used with caution is generally applicable.

Let me give an example. Perhaps the biggest divergency occurs in the scholars who come from the Young-Luther approach. They concentrate upon the earliest writings of Luther when he was still in the monastery, and find a doctrine of justification in which the sinner is not only declared righteous but is *made* righteous, so that justification depends partly upon the good works of the believer. Their view rests upon two assumptions: that Luther's reformational doctrine emerged before 1518, and that the later doctrine of forensic justification in the Lutheran Confessions was a divergency or even corruption of Luther. It is a fact that in his late writings, and especially in his autobiographical *Preface* of 1545,[7] Luther repudiated his early teaching and propounded forensic justification in a manner which agrees completely with the teaching of the Confessions. How are we to proceed with this hermeneutical problem? Some have attempted to avoid the issue by insisting that the Young and the Mature Luther fully agree; an example of this is the editor of the *Lectures on Romans* in the American Edition.[8] This procedure is not acceptable. Some of us solve the problem as follows. The early writings of Luther are pre-Reformational and have chiefly historic interest. We must accept his retractions from the later years and especially form the *Preface* of 1545; in full accord with this are the forensic teachings on justification in the *Lectures on Galatians* and *Lectures on Genesis* from the last fifteen years of his life. However, the majority of Luther scholars would take the opposing position. Leading spokesmen have said that Luther's later retractions came from his old age when senility was already setting in, that his dating of the "evangelical discovery" at late 1518 or early 1519 is erroneous, and that those of us who find an agreement on justification between Luther and the Confessions are guilty of proceeding form a position of their theological or ecclesial bias. "The trouble with you, Green, is that you are biased; you approach Luther from the prejudiced position of the Lutheran Church and its Confessions; we are unbiases because we reject that position." Now, actually, the position of my opponents may well be fully as "biased"; my assumption is that the Lutheran Confessions are a useful summary of the teaching of Luther and his successors, and their assumption is the opposite. Students of hermeneutics today generally agree that no one is without a bias, and that the most insidious and dangerous bias is the one that is denied. As we proceed, however, I shall attempt to show the my position (assumtions, "bias") actually accords with the facts.

A sound hermeneutics of Luther research must be fully historical in approach and fully systematical in orientation. It must be fully systematical, else the researcher will completely pass over the theological point involved, overlook the profound, and dwell upon the obvious or trivial. And yet, the criticism is not unjust that, too often, Luther studies have gone out excessively from preconceived theological notions which have prejudiced the results and blinded the researcher to the real Luther. Luther interpretation must be fully historical. It must place Luther squarely within his historical situation, it must study his life and works in relation to their historical context, and it must subject itself to the canons of historical criticism.

Now, how do we interpret the Lutheran Confessions? We often speak of the distinction between the *quatenus* and the *quia* subscription of the symbols. If we subscribe them in the sense of *quatenus*, which means "insofar as," we are saying that we confess these teachings *insofar as* they agree with the Scriptures; if we subscribe them in the sense of *quia*, "because," we are saying that we subscribe to these writings *because* we have discovered that they actually agree throughout with the Holy Scriptures. The *quatenus* subscription is not very meaningful; a Unitarian or a Christian Scientist could accept whatever part of the Confessions he found in accord with his understanding of what Holy Writ teaches. Therefore, Lutherans usually speak of the *quia* subscription, which implies that they have studied both the Sacred Scriptures and the Lutheran Confessions, that they have found that the Confessions agree with the teachings of the Bible, and that they accept them *because* of this agreement.

However, what we have just said about subscription of the Confessions leaves a lot of unanswered questions until we have laid down some principles of how to interpret them. The hermeneutics of the Lutheran symbols is a problem which has not been taken seriously enough. We might suggest several basic procedures.

1) It is essential to study the Confessions in their original languages. The *crux interpretatum* demands consulting the original German or Latin just as much as Biblical studies require the knowledge of Hebrew and Greek. There is no satisfactory translation of the *Book of Concord* available in English. Besides a number of serious mistranslations in the version edited by Theodore G. Tappert, this version, instead of translating verses from Luther's

German Bible directly into English, supplied instead the renditions of the *Revised Standard Version,* which sometimes resulted in serious descrepancies.[9]

2) The Confessions must be studied historically. A. They must be studied within the context in which they were written. The *Augustana* was written to show that Lutheranism is truly catholic and entitled to legal recognition within the Holy Roman Empire, the catechisms were written for instructing the common people, and the *Formula of Concord* was written to draw the line between Lutheranism and Crypto-Calvinism, among other things. In interpreting Luther's assertion in the *Schmalkald Articles* that the pope is the Antichrist, we must ask questions such as the following: did he say the "papacy" or the "pope," which pope did he mean, why did he think that the pope had the marks of the Antichrist, does the pope today have those marks, and how well did his remark agree with the Sacred Scriptures? Is his assertion an infallible teaching or a personal opinion? B. The Confessions must be studied according to the principles of historical criticism. This means, first, that we ascertain the most accurate textual readings. It means, second, that we study the various written and oral traditions which preceded the present texts. For example, we need to read Luther's earlier catechetical writings and catechetical sermons in order to understand the catechisms, or, in interpreting the *Formula of Concord,* we must check out the affirmations of such forerunners as the *Six Sermons* of Andreae, the *Swabian-Saxon Concord,* the *Maulbronn Formula,* and the *Torgau Book.* Since the *Formula* refers to certain writings of Luther, we have to be acquainted with these in order to understand the *Formula.* C. Studying the Confessions historically also means that we treat each of the Symbols individually and that we study the private theology of their writers as well as the later formulations. Especially important, beside Luther, are Melanchthon, Chemnitz, Chytraeus, and Andreae.

3) The Confessions should be interpreted in such a way that we distinguish between the doctrine that was being presented and the form in which it was developed. Thus, the particular exegesis of a certain passage is not necessarily "binding"; otherwise, the Confessions would become the norm of the Scriptures rather than the

Bible being the judge of the Confessions. One's loyalty to the Confessions is not thrown into question simply because one does not agree that when garlic is rubbed over a magnet it loses its magnetic qualities, or that a hot iron is the combination of the two elements of earth and fire.

No less a Confessional leader than Carl Ferdinand Wilhelm Walther insisted that a full subscription does not call for acknowledging the validity of every analogy used to support the Confessions in the sixteenth century. Walther insisted that no man was fit for the pastoral office who lacked competencies in studying the Confessions, and demanded an unconditional subscription to all who asked to be received into the Lutheran ministry. But he acknowledged that such an acceptance was limited to the doctrinal content of the symbolical books,[10] and he added: ''The servant of the Church is not bound to follow the form, the method, and the process of proof used in the Symbols and to avoid any other.''[11]

I take it that this is what Friedrich Brunstaed meant with his distinction between *Lehrintention* or doctrinal intention and *Lehrform*, the manner in which the doctrine is presented and supported.[12] Someone might voice the fear that we are leaving the door open for excessive liberty. However, this argument is not conclusive. Any hermeneutical rule can be violated. The teachings themselves must be firmly adhered to, but the manner of presentation of the sixteenth century will at times be dropped for a more convincing one today.

In our discussion of the hermeneutics of Luther, we noted the need for historical criticism, both lower and higher, and we established the principle that his later works, coming after his full apprehension of Reformational insights, should provide the norm for evaluating his early teachings. Under hermeneutics of the Confessions, we considered the linguistic problems, the importance of the historical context, and the need to distinguish between form and content. We must now refer to the following question: To what extent is our knowledge of Luther to guide our interpretation of the Confessions, and how far shall our knowledge of the Confessions influence our interpretation of Luther? We see examples of errors on both sides. There are the Luther scholars who ignore

Lutheranism, and there are Lutherans who merely read into Luther their own preconceived ideas as Confessional churchmen. We shall try to avoid these pitfalls as we proceed to examine examples where there is divergency as well as convergence between Luther and the Confessions.

II. Divergencies Between the Young Luther and the Confessions

It is not surprising that divergencies are to be found between the Early Luther and the Confessions, for the same disparities exist also between the Young and the Mature Luther. We have already taken note of the difference in his doctrine of justification. Another example, from his first *Lectures on the Psalter* (1513-15), is his generous recognition to Neo-Platonic thought with its questionable dualism of the flesh and the spirit as a splitting apart of body and soul. Many scholars have regarded the Ninety-Five Theses of 1517 as "Reformational," but if we approach them with fresh eyes we shall see that Luther at that time was not "rebelling" against the pope; in fact, he anathemized all who interfered with the sale of the indulgences.[13] A year after the alleged posting of the Ninety-Five Theses, Luther still regarded the authority of the Roman Church above that of the Bible, he held daily masses for the living and the dead, he gave out indulgences to the people, he taught the existence of purgatory, he followed the mediaeval teaching of transubstantiation, he venerated the Blessed Virgin Mary, and he invoked the saints.[14] Therefore, we must exert greater caution in quoting from the Young Luther than many have done in the past. And since Luther rejected his early teachings later on, we shall be more careful about playing him against the Lutheran Confessions.

III. Differences in the Doctrine of Revelation

Luther's theology had reached its mature form by 1525. In that year he wrote *De servo arbitrio*, commonly translated *The Bondage of the Will*. Luther regarded this in later years as his best book; nevertheless, the Lutheran Church has never fully accepted this book nor been able to learn from it. Perhaps one reason has been the erroneous notion that *The Bondage of the Will* was written about predestination, or even that Luther taught double predestination like Calvin; both notions are highly inaccurate, as we shall presently see.

In line with his distinction of Law and Gospel, Luther held that individual piety as well as theological scholarship should avoid speculations about God in his majestic attributes such as transcendence, power, wisdom, beauty, judging, etc., and should go out from his merciful attributes—immanence, humiliation, mercy, kindness, forgiving—instead. He stated in the *Commentary on Galatians:* "Theology that is Christian and true, as I often warn, does not emphasize God in majesty, like Moses and other teachings, but it emphasizes Christ born of the Virgin, our Mediator and High Priest."[15] He pointed out how Paul connected Jesus Christ with God the Father, and continued: "Thereby, he teaches us the Christian religion, which does not begin from the top *(non a summo)* like all other religions, but from below *(sed ab imo)*." Luther now applied this axiom to piety and scholarship: "Wherefore, when you want to think and act in regard to your salvation, then avoid speculations of the majesty, avoid all thoughts of works, of traditions, of philosophy, and of the Law of God, but turn yourself quickly to the manger and the Mother's womb. Embrace this infant, this tiny boy of the Virgin. Look at him being born, being nursed, going about among people, teaching, dying, rising from the dead, borne up above all heavens, holding power over all things." Luther now concludes that this procedure, in which theology avoids speculations about the majestic or Hidden God *(Deus absconditus)* and goes out instead from his self-revelation in Christ *(Deus revelatus)*, will keep the believer and the theologian "in the right way," *in via recta.*[16]

Calvin did not follow Luther's Christological approach to revelation, but taught instead a Pneumatological doctrine. For Luther, revelation was a man, Jesus Christ; for Calvin, revelation was a "Sacred Oracle" which came straight down from heaven under the inspiration of the Holy Spirit and recorded in a book, the Bible.[17] The later theology of Lutheran Orthodoxy did not follow Luther's Christocentric approach but modified its understanding of revelation and the Word after Calvin. Later Lutherans tended, like Calvin, to neglect the distinction of Law and Gospel and the difference between the Old and New Testaments. Law and Gospel lost their rightful place in the Prolegomena of Dogmatics as the principle of the entire system, and instead were relegated to the third part, Pneumatology. In this shifting around, room was made for the concept of "natural revelation" in juxtaposition to the Bible, that is, a distinction between revelation learned from reason and revelation by inspiration of the Spirit. The doctrine of the Word had changed from a Christological to a Pneumatological one.[18]

It is often assumed that the theology of Lutheran Orthodoxy after 1600 faithfully followed Luther and the Confessions, but, as we have just seen, it departed from the Christological understanding of the Word. Hence, it is not surprising that its understanding of the doctrine of God in Luther and the Confessions was also defective. Although the Young Luther had at times applauded that sixth-century mystic philosopher, Pseudo-Dionysius the Areopagite, the Mature Luther was very critical of him. The seventeenth-century dogmaticians, however, returned to his three ways of coming to knowledge of God by the use of reason: the way of negation, the way of eminence, and the way of causality.[19] These scholars went on to describe God as a series of "attributes" (a "divine attribute" was a quality man ascribed to God), qualities likewise derived by use of reason. In setting up the lists of attributes, they neglected to divide them into those dealing with the majestic and the merciful qualities of God, a further confusion of Law and Gospel.[20] But no matter how earnestly they strove to divulge information about God which He had not chosen to reveal about himself, their best efforts could only lead them to *Deus absconditus*, God Hidden in the Law. Any notion that they were proceeding beyond God's self-revelation in Christ and his self-disclosure in the Bible was a self-delusion.

The notion of a natural theology became prominent under Rationalism and the Enlightenment, the Romanticism and theology of feeling in Friedrich Schleiermacher, the holiness movement of John Wesley, Charles Finney, and their successors, and Neo-Pentecostalism. Among some Lutherans in North America, enthusiasm, stemming perhaps from Jean Jacques Rousseau's social-contract theory and democratistic notions, had led to concepts which need to be examined critically. Does the Holy Spirit really speak through the majority-vote of parliamentary assemblies? Are such gatherings really able to claim authoritative interpretations of the Bible because of a direct revelation manifested in the balloting? Does the local congregation really "possess" certain inherent spiritual gifts which it, in turn, confers or "transfers" to its pastors? Are these ideas genuine examples of Lutheran thinking, or invasions of some of the aforementioned notions?

IV. **The Problem of the "Universal Saving Will of God"**

One of the difficult questions in theology is this: Why are so many lost when Christ died for all? Calvin settled that problem by teaching that Christ died only for the predestined; God willed for them to go to heaven, and for the rest, he willed an eternity in hell. Both Melanchthon and Luther recoiled from such a double predestination. Melanchthon felt that God willed all to be saved, and the fact that many were not saved was due to some defect in the individual. Thus, Melanchthon became the father of the concept of God's universal will for salvation, which became characteristic of Lutheranism. Luther, the monergist, travelled a different route. It is noteworthy that in his Bible translation he did not translate I Tim. 2:4: "God will have all men to be saved," but "Welcher wil/ das allen Menschen geholffen werde." In a comment on this passage from 1525, he said that the words "to be saved" did not mean that God willed all men to achieve eternal salvation: "The words, *salvum facere [sozein]*, recur often in the Gospel, and mean to thrive or receive help, not to become eternally blessed. Therefore, the expression does not have to do only with eternal life, but it embraces all help, temporal and eternal, and declares that he is the only Saviour, through whom are helped, whether pious or evil, man or beast. He wills that they all should thrive, wherever they need his help."[21] In these comments he took up a concept which reappeared the same year in *The Bondage of the Will*. The papists err when they quote the words, "God will have all men to be saved," as though God willed the salvation of all people, and then they say that it depends upon you and me, and upon our free will, whether or not this will of God shall be done. As Luther went on, he took a position that subsequent Lutherans have generally not followed. He made this comment on I Tim.

2:4: "A few will ask: If it is true that God wills such a thing, why then does it not happen, that everyone becomes blessed? If it is our will that hinders, then it must be stronger than God's will, which cannot cause what he wills to happen if we are not willing. Now God has said in Isaiah 46 [:10]: 'My counsel shall stand, and all my will shall be done.' Thus Rom. 9 [:19]: 'Who can oppose his will?' Thus he proves it many times that he can awaken the whole world, to oppose his will, in order that one my see that his will shall be done. How, then, can one make this fit with the notion that I can prevent and hinder my eternal salvation, if it is really God's will? Accordingly, one must not conclude what they say; otherwise one would immediately have to conclude, that our will were stronger than the will of God.''[22] Luther said much the same thing in *The Bondage of the Will.* One was basically dealing with the question "whether…[man] has 'free-will' God-ward, that God should obey man and do what man wills, or whether God has not rather a free will with respect to man, that man should will and do what God wills….''[23] Luther went to great pains to establish the supremacy of God's will and the total inability of man to move himself in the things of the Holy Ghost: "…a man cannot be thoroughly humbled till he realizes that his salvation is utterly beyond his own powers, counsels, efforts, will and works, and depends absolutely on the choice, counsel, pleasure, and work of Another—God alone.''[24] This humbling is necessary for him to be saved. Faith deals with things that cannot be seen but are hidden: "That there may be room for faith, therefore, all things that are believed must be hidden. Moreover, nothing is more thoroughly hidden than when it is under its contrary appearance, sense, or trial. Accordingly, when God makes alive, he does it by putting to death; when he justifies, he does so by accusing one guilty; when he carries to heaven, he does it by dragging down to hell….In this way God conceals his eternal loving-kindness and mercy under eternal wrath, his righteousness under iniquity. This is the highest grade of faith—to believe that he is compassionate who saves so few and damns so many, to believe that he is just who by his own will makes us unavoidably damnable….If therefore I were able by any power of reason to comprehend how this God is merciful and just who displays such wrath and unfavorableness, there would be no need for faith."[25] Thus, we see that it is a matter of Law and Gospel, of God Hidden and Revealed. The Law shows God's wrath against sin; Luther says that God in his wrath, his hidden nature or his majesty "neither deplores death nor takes it away, but works life, death, and all things in all things."[26] Strictly speaking, God is not revealed but hidden in the Law. It is only in the Gospel that we learn to know the innermost being of God. This is learned when we see God in Christ, reconciling the world unto himself (II Cor. 5). Luther says that we must not busy ourselves with the hidden counsels of God; we are not to pry into the God of majesty.[27] But we are to occupy ourselves with God incarnate, that is, with Jesus crucified, who procured our salvation. In this God, hidden in majesty and the Law, but revealed in mercy and the Gospel, we have it all. "It is the same God who becomes incarnate, weeps, laments, and groans over the perdition of the ungodly, whenever the will of his majesty passes over and rejects others according to his purpose, so that they perish."[28] Luther then says that we have no right to question God or to pry into his secret purposes, but that we should rather stand in awe of him who can will and do such things. (Calvin solved this problem, instead, with the doctrine of double predestination.)

How did the *Formula of Concord* stand to this powerful statement of Luther? These words might seem like a contradiction of Luther and the acceptance of Melanchthon's concept of a universal will of God unto salvation: "It is not the will of God that anyone should be condemned, but that all men should be converted unto him and become eternally blessed."[29] We might be confirmed in the opinion that this was the intrusion of Melanchthonism when we observe that these words were written by the favorite pupil of Melanchthon, David Chytraeus.[30] Yet, the discrepancy is only apparent. For Luther, it was only the *Deus absconditus* who neither deplored the death of the sinner nor took it away; Chytraeus was following Luther's instructions when he said that we do not have to do with such a hidden God, but with God revealed in Christ. In the immediate context, Chytraeus quoted John 3:16 and pointed out that God had sent forth the public preaching of the Gospel. Accordingly, the *Formula of Concord* chose to present only *Deus revelatus*, God revealed in his Son, "God preached."[31] God hid-

95

den was disregarded. The concerns of Luther were presented in other language in Article 5 of the Formula, "On Law and Gospel." It belonged to a later generation to forsake Luther's distinction of God hidden and revealed, of Law and Gospel, and to replace it with a concept of revelation based upon a Book rather than upon the Son of God. One might wish that the Formulators had referred more clearly and explicitly to *The Bondage of the Will;* it seems to have been cited explicitly only three times in the Formula. Nevertheless, they kept Luther's heritage when they stated impressively the proper distinction of Law and Gospel.

V. A Comparison in the Doctrine of Justification

Luther's doctrine of justification was a drawing of the consequences from his distinction of Law and Gospel. Luther, who in his *The Bondage of the Will* had excluded any kind of human cooperation in the establishment of faith, could afford to emphasize justification by faith. But Melanchthon held a doctrine of the will with a dual orientation upon the helpless will of unregenerate man and the active will of regenerate man. This made it necessary for him to be painfully scrupulous to avoid synergism. This likewise required caution in teaching justification by faith, and led Melanchthon to prefer speaking of justification by grace, which meant being overpowered by the favor or benevolence of God. Whereas Christ was the content of justifying faith in Luther, in Melanchthon faith was the acceptance of the promises of the Gospel which experienced the imputation of the passive righteousness of Christ. To speak of a contradiction between the two reformers is unnecessary. But to obscure the differences is to lose the richness of the twofold approach, and to overlook the intellectualisation toward which Melanchthon's theology tended to veer. To speak of justification as the imputation of the righteousness of Christ to the believing sinner was characteristic of Melanchthon, but Luther sometimes used the same way of speaking. Yet it was not Luther's distinctive manner of expression. Justification did not mean appropriating something out of a doctrine but it meant having Christ take over one's life.[32] The *Formula* teaches: "...A poor sinner is justified before God...without any merit or worthiness on our part, and without any preceding, present, or subsequent works, by sheer grace...."[33] This formulation is taken directly out of the first edition of the *Loci communes* of Melanchthon.[34] The *Formula* continues in these words which seem to echo Luther: "For faith does not justify because it is so good a work and so God-pleasing a virtue, but because it lays hold on and accepts the merit of Christ in the promise of the holy Gospel. This merit has to be applied to us and to be made our own through faith if we are to be justified thereby. Therefore, the righteousness which by grace is reckoned to faith or to the believers is the obedience, the passion, and the resurrection of Christ when he satisfied the law for us and paid for our sin."[35]

VI. The Lord's Supper and Christology

Luther and Melanchthon had both agreed that in the Holy Supper, through the sacramental union, the body and blood of Christ are truly united with the bread and wine and, through them, are given to all who eat and drink. When Luther debated with Zwingli at Marburg in 1529, it became apparent that their differences were not confined to the sacrament, but that behind the sacrament stood an even more crucial divergency on the doctrine of Christ. Behind the variant Christologies lurked two radically different ideologies: Luther's understanding of Christ was strongly Biblical, whereas Zwingli's doctrine bore the stamp of the Neo-Platonic dualism of matter and spirit. Luther went out from the proposition that God had revealed himself in the man Jesus of the four gospels, and that God was fully present in the Babe of Bethlehem and the Man of Calvary. Zwingli, and Calvin later on, limited both the divine qualities of Jesus and the miraculous element of the Holy Supper in line with their maxim, the finite cannot contain the infinite. Luther realized that the greatest danger was not to the sacrament but to the doctrine of Christ itself. When the Reformed said that the body and blood of Jesus could not be present in the sacrament because these were confined to heaven, Luther countered that the divine nature of Christ imparted to his human nature the ability to be omnipresent (*communicatio idiomatum*). When the Reformed said that Christ could not be bodily present in the sacrament because he had ascended to the right hand of God, Luther replied that the right hand of God is everywhere, and therefore Christ can be present in many places at the same time, just as God is omnipresent. The Latin word of everywhere is *ubique,* and the ugly word *ubiquitas* or ubiquity, literally, everywhereness, was used as a term of scorn by his Reformed opponents. Melanchthon winced at bad Latin and refused to use the word or the concept, although he taught the communication of the divine properties to the human nature of Christ. Luther felt that the Christological argument was very important in explaining the scriptural doctrine of the Supper according to his understanding. Melanchthon disagreed, and wrote down these words on March 16, 1546: "De Vbiquitate non est disputandum, In hac controuersia est longa alia res, Nec Scholastici quicquam dicunt de Vbiquitate, Sed retinent simplicem sententiam de Corporali praesencia Christi."[36] This may be translated as follows: "Concerning ubiquity there must be no disputation; the problem in this controversy is a completely different matter. Nor did any of the schoolmen speak concerning ubiquity, but they retained the simple understanding of the corporal presence of Christ."[37] Now, there was nothing wrong in Melanchthon refusing to use the doctrine of the ubiquity in teaching the sacrament, and we applaud his insistence that the corporal presence of Christ be taught. Nevertheless, Luther was right when he linked the sacrament to Christology. One of the strange quirks in history concerns the sequel to that memorandum of Melanchthon. The Gnesio-Lutherans, the ultra conservative party who opposed Melanchthon, rejected the Wittenberg edition of the collected works of Luther on the ground that its contents had been tampered with by pupils of Melanchthon; therefore, they edited the new Jena edition of Luther's works, which they supposed to have gotten back to the authentic texts. But they mistook Melanchthon's memorandum on ubiquity and published it as an authentic statement of Luther. Misled by their own error in textual criticism, the Gnesio-Lutherans took the position that the doctrine of the Holy Supper must be drawn exclusively from the words of institution, without developing the sacrament out of the doctrine of the omnipresence of Christ.

When the *Formula of Concord* was framed in the 1570s, most of the participants from both parties were willing to write the article on the Holy Supper with little reference to Christology.[38] The immediately following article was then devoted to Christology, neatly separated from the sacrament. However, the south Germans had adhered to Luther's teaching on ubiquity, and one of their number, Jacob Andreae, was the principal organizer of the peace effort. The first draft of Article 7 was written by David Chytraeus, a disciple of Melanchthon, and his version concentrated on the Words of Institution and avoided Christology. Subsequently, Andreae insisted on adding five paragraphs[39] which quoted a strongly Christological statement of Luther; not to be outdone, Chytraeus then extended the quotation.[40] Accordingly, Article 7 of the *Formula of Concord* struck a balance between the views of Luther and Melanchthon. It follows Melanchthon when it teaches that the true body and blood of Christ are present "in, with, and under" the bread and wine; and it follows Luther when it links the sacrament to the omnipresence of the God-man and says concerning the outward elements—this is the true body and blood of Christ.

Conclusion

It is important for Luther scholars to consider the sequel his teachings experienced in subsequent Lutheranism. Such later developments supply an historical context to Luther and his times which may or may not truly reflect his intentions. His successors wanted to be true to Luther and his Gospel. How well they succeeded is an important subject for further research. At this time, careful investigations are required in respect to Luther, the Confessions, their interrelationship, and the right or wrong interpretations of later Lutherans as well as scholars of other churchly persuasions. So far as the Lutheran Church is concerned, it needs to sharpen its focus and intensify its knowledge of the relation between Luther and the Confessions. It needs to become aware of how it has moved away from its "chief teacher," and to recover some lost insights. This is not because it was said by Luther, but because or insofar as it accords with the Sacred Scriptures and leads the church to a fuller appreciation and proclamation of the Gospel of Jesus Christ.

ENDNOTES

1. S D, Rule and Norm, 5.

2. Ibid., §9.

3. S D 7:34.

4. S D 7:41.

5. S D 2:44, 89.

6. The hermeneutics of research into Luther and the Confessions has been practiced widely but only seldom subjected to scholarly analysis. A good historical study of various interpretations of Luther is presented in Horst Stephan, *Luther in den Wandlungen seiner Kirche* (Berlin: Alfred Toepelmann, 1951). Cf. Heinrich Bornkamm, *Luther im Spiegel der deutschen Geistesgeschichte* (Goettingen: Vandenhoeck & Ruprecht, 1970). See also my discussion "Historiographical Prolegomena" in my book, *How Melanchthon Helped Luther Discover the Gospel* (Fallbrook, Calif.: Verdict Publications, 1980), pp. 31-59. Cf. also Friedrich Wilhelm Kantzenbach, "Modelle knofessioneller Hermeneutik und die Funktion der Konkordienformel im Neuluthertum," in Wenzel Lohff and Lewis W. Spitz, eds., *Widerspruch, Dialog und Dinigung* (Stuttgart: Calwer Verlag, 1977), pp. 277-296. The hermeneutics of the Confessions is further discussed in my book, *The Formula of Concord: An Historiographical and Bibliographical Guide*, Sixteenth Century Bibliography, 11 (St. Louis: Center for Reformation Research, 1977).

7. WA 54:179-187; LW 34:327-338.

8. LW 25.

9. The critical edition which must be used for scholarly purposes is *Die Bekenntnisschriften der evangelisch-lutherischen Kirche, Herausgegeben im Gedenkjahr der Augsburgischen Konfession 1930* (Goettingen: Vandenhoeck & Ruprecht, 1930 ff.). Even this excellent edition needs revision. The most widely used English translation is *The Book of Concord*, ed. by Theodore G. Tappert *et al.* (Philadelphia: Fortress Press, 1959). The important documents which precursed the several confessions are hardly available in critical editions.

10. Carl Ferdinand Wilhelm Walther, "Why Should Our Pastors, Teachers and Professors Subscribe Unconditionally to the Symbolic Writings of Our Church?" *Concordia Theological Monthly*, 18(April, 1947):241-242.

11. Ibid., p. 242.

12. Friedrich Brunstaed, *Theologie der lutherischen Bekenntnisschriften* (Guetersloh: C. Bertelsmann Verlag, 1951), p. 9.

13. WA 1:236:35-36, 236:39-40, 237:3-4; LW 31:31; Theses 69;71;73.

14. Green, *How Melanchthon Helped Luther,* p. 65.

15. WA 40,I:77:11-13; LW 26:28-29.

16. WA 40,I:80:13-14; LW 26:30-31.

17. There is comparatively little in Calvin of Luther's concept that divine revelation took place in Christ; he like to go forth instead from the impenetrable majesty and sovereignty of God. *Institutes of the Christian Religion:* ''...the Scriptures obtain full authority among believers only when men regard them as having sprung from heaven, as if there the living words of God were heard'' (Philadelphia: The Westminster Press, 1960), The Library of Christian Classics, 20:74. Calvin went out from above rather than below when he called the Word a Sacred Oracle, L C C, 20:71-72, 21:1157, 1178, 1189, 1214, etc. Whereas Luther's understanding of the Word was soteriological, Calvin's tended toward the cognitive; not so much Christ, as the Holy Ghost, speaks when we read the Holy Book today, cf. L C C 20:81. A leading concept of Calvin was the testimony of the Holy Spirit, L C C 20:78-80, *et passim.*

18. A striking example of this is the reference of Johann Wilhelm Baier, *Compendium Theologiae Positivae,* 1694, new ed. (Berlin: Schlawitz, 1864) to Hebr. 1:1-2 in his discussion of revelation and Holy Scriptures in Prolegomena 2:1a, p. 43. He develops four ways in which God has made himself known (by way of patriarchs, dreams, visions, and direct inspiration as in II Tim. 3:17, and II Pt. 1:21), without mentioning that God's final word was spoken by his Son, Hebr. 1:2. In developing the doctrine of verbal inspiration, the seventeenth-century dogmaticians tended to lose the Christocentrism of Luther and veer into a pneumatological doctrine of the Word. Perhaps this was a precursor of modern Neo-Pentecostalism. This is not to reject inspiration but to warn against a doctrine of the Word which is separated from Christology and neutral to the distinction of Law and Gospel.

19. Mediaeval theologians had followed Pseudo-Dionysius the Areopagite in a natural theology of the divine attributes based upon the three *viae:* the *via eminentiae,* the *via negationis,* and the via causalitatis. This was explicitly present in David Hollaz, *Examen theologicum acroamaticum* (Stargard, 1707) I:295-296. This method is still visible in Franz Pieper, *Christian Dogmatics* (St. Louis: Concordia Publ. House, 1924, 1959), I:435.

20. Although Pieper follows the old dogmaticians in dividing the "attributes" into negative and positive ones, he breaks through the system, with its obfuscation of the distinction between the majestic and the merciful attributes (Law and Gospel). He abserves that those attributes which speak of the unity, infinity, omniscience, omnipotence, and omnipresence could only terrify us, and he points to the all-important character of God in his grace, "the center of the entire Scriptures" (*Christian Dogmatics,* I:437). More of this in my forthcoming Dogmatics.

21. Johann Georg Walch, ed., *D. Martin Luthers...Saemtliche Schriften,* 2nd ed. (St. Louis: Concordia Publ. House, 1880-1910) 9:579.

22. Ibid., 9:577-578.

23. WA 18:781:10-12; Martin Luther, *The Bondage of the Will,* trans. by J.I. Packer and O.R. Johnston (Westwood, N.J.: Fleming H. Revell, 1957), p. 310, subsequently referred to as "P J"; cf. LW 33:285.

24. WA 18:632:30-32; Otto Clemen, ed., *Luthers Werke in Auswahl* (Bonn: A. Marcus and E. Weber's Verlag, 1925), 3:123, subsequently referred to as "Cl"; cf. P J p. 100; cf LW 33:62.

25. WA 18:633:7-11, 14-17, 19-21; Cl 3:124; cf. P J p. 101; cf. LW 33:62-63.

26. WA 18:685:21-23; Cl 3:177; cf. P J p. 170; cf. LW 33:140.

27. WA 18:689:18-22; Cl 3:182; cf. P J p. 176; cf. LW 33:145-146.

28. WA 18:689:32-33,690:1; Cl 3:182; cf. P J p. 176; cf. LW 33:146.

29. S D 2:49.

30. See George J. Fritschel, *The Formula of Concord: Its Origin and Contents* (Philadelphia: The Lutheran Publication Society, 1916), p. 147.

31. Luther wrote: "...de Deo vel voluntate Dei nobis praedicata, revelata, oblata, culta." WA 18:685:3-4; Cl 3:177; P J p. 170; LW 33:139.

32. For documentation, see my book *How Melanchthon Helped Luther,* pp. 253-267.

33. S D 3:9.

34. *Melanchthons Werke in Auswahl* (Guetersloh: Guetersloher Verlagshaus Gerd Mohn, 1978), II,1:108:27ff.

35. S D 3:13-14.

36. WA 48:236:8-11; C R 9:1087-1088.

37. See Theodor Mahlmann, *Das neue Dogma der lutherischen Christologie* (Guetersloh: Guetersloher Verlagshaus Gerd Mohn, 1969), pp. 19-43. This is also discussed in my chapter on S D 7, pp. 213-216, 307, in Robert D. Preus and Wilbert H. Rosin, eds., *A Contemporary Look at the Formula of Concord* (St. Louis: Concordia Publ. House, 1978).

38. Art. 7.

39. S D 7:93-97.

40. §§99-103.

V LUTHER'S COURAGE OF FAITH

by
Egil Grislis

Luther's personal courage has never been doubted by his admirers and has been appropriately rehearsed during this year of 1983.[1] But just what accounted for Luther's great courage? Was Luther born courageous? Or did he need to struggle with himself repeatedly and only slowly come to acquire the rare virtue of courage? What role did grace play in the formation of this courage? How was Luther's faith related to his courage? Indeed, would Luther have been a courageous man even without his eventual grasp of the justification by grace through faith?

I.

Without attempting to answer all possible questions about Luther's courage, we shall begin by noting that Luther was well aware of how really dangerous it was to attempt to reform the

103

church. Had not his immediate superiors, stunned by fear, delivered their warning, and asked him "not to bring disgrace upon our order..."?[2]

Luther did not question the accuracy of this common sense advice. At the same time, he did not heed the warning, but merely admitted with a remarkable calmness: "Anyone who is supposed to criticize the whole world—emperors, kings, princes, wise men, learned men—and say that their way of life is damned before God, has to stick his neck out."[3] And he knew, as we do, what happens to necks that have been stuck out! Still, Luther did what he believed to be his religious duty, which at Worms he formulated in one summary sentence: "I cannot do otherwise, here I stand, may God help me, Amen."[4] And in retrospect Luther assured, without any doubt, with complete accuracy: "If I had known that as many devils as there were tiles on the roofs at Worms took aim at me, I would still have entered the city...."[5]

What was the root of such a strict, and courageous, understanding of his duty? Did he conceive of his mission as completely predetermined? Or, did even Luther search for his way, waver and doubt?

Luther's courage was certainly not blind. He did not find himself automatically proclaiming the truth—he had to struggle for it. And at times the inward struggle was very hard indeed. At Worms the Catholic emperor, Charles V, had asked plainly and powerfully: "Can a single impotent monk be wiser than the whole world?"[6] This was a question which could not be readily forgotten. Even years later it gnawed, even burned, deep within Luther's conscience.[7] Then Luther did not hesitate to admit, in courage confessing his fears: "How often did my heart quail, punish me, and reproach me with its single strongest argument: Are you the only wise man? Can it be that all the others are in error and have erred for so long a time? What is you are mistaken and lead so many people into error who might all be eternally damned?"[8]

Luther's reformation was not carried out without genuine tribulations—those well known *Anfechtungen*—in the midst of which Luther struggles with himself and came to know the very depth of despair. Thus, quite clearly, Luther's courage was not due to an optimistic assumption that he is somehow invulnerable or indestructible. Luther knew that the odds were against him, that most likely he would be burned at the stake as a heretic. On occasion Luther recorded echoes of the kind of debates that had gone on in his soul: "'They can murder you!' 'Then what? Can they revive me and kill me again? Or perhaps devour my body like a tasty morsel? They can't and won't kill me unless my Lord permits it and tells me so.'"[9] It is tempting simply to conclude that in the very end Luther's faith proved to be stronger than his fears. In a sense such indeed had been the case. But Luther's own explanation assigned to his tribulations a far more positive role. Luther noted that only when he became totally aware of his own utter helplessness, was he able to rely fully on the help of the Word of God.[10] Luther admitted: "It is as if God were saying: 'You must be weary and emptied, so that there is no way out for you. Then I will give you strength. First you must become nothing, then consolation and strength will come.' This happened to me, Martin Luther, who against my will came up against the whole world, and then God helped me."[11]

In other words, Luther became a successful reformer not because he was prepared to defy the whole world, but rather because, having failed to find security in self-reliance, Luther relied on God the Almighty! It is precisely in this specific context where Luther needed to speak so disparagingly of reason—that is, the so-called "realistic" assessment of the actual situation. Luther confessed: "As for me, Martin Luther, unless God had closed for me the eyes of reason, I would long ago have stopped preaching and have despaired. Now a boldness, or certainty, comes to my aid."[12] Luther made the same point when he, a religious activist, warned of a reliance on mere human efforts. Luther now knew that in the last analysis only divine wisdom and intervention can offer authentic help.[13] Indeed, to refer to divine wisdom actually meant to acknowledge that it was not in one's own possession. Luther admitted without any further hesitation: "And I, Martin Luther, know that I am still feeble. Many think that they have faith when they have made a specter of faith for themselves, but when they meet danger, they slip."[14] Luther did not slip; he stood stalwart in courage.

Without pride or posturing, Luther pointed to faith and explained how he understood faith: "The art of faith consists in this, that we apprehend what we do not see. In fact, all that we have from Christ is hidden from view; what we see is its opposite. Faith sees the intangible, that which is not felt or apprehended. That is the skill of faith. It has sharp vision, enabling me to perceive life when death stares me in the face, when I see the executioner beheading me or burning me at the stake, and when I am being killed. All this I see and feel, and yet faith also sees life and says: 'Even though I am being killed, I shall live again.'" Is it not almost painfully obvious that this definition of faith is autobiographical? Luther had inwardly shuddered at the thought of his, most likely, very speedy execution. Yet when all outward support had failed, he had found the presence of God to be his assurance and source of courage!

In subsequent years, Luther, the Scripture scholar, discovered that such a divine grooming into faith had been widely shared by the true believers of all ages. Faith always blossomed in utter loneliness and bore courage in life's greatest storms.

II.

There were Scriptural texts and stories that convinced Luther that he had not used his autobiography to invent a doctrine of faith. Rather, his own life had merely helped him to discover what was already in the texts of the Holy Scriptures, ever true and ever to be seen by all who would look in faith. Luther wrote: "Do we not read in the Old Testament that God generally raised up only one prophet at a time? Moses was alone during the exodus from Egypt. Elijah was alone in King Ahab's day. After him, Elisha stood alone. Isaiah was alone in Jerusalem, Hosea alone in Israel, Jeremiah alone in Judea, Ezekiel alone in Babylon, and so it went. Even though they had many disciples called 'children of the prophets,' God never allowed more than one man alone to preach and rebuke the people."[16] In other words, God did not ever intend that faith would be made easy and be bolstered with a majority support. Faith and its expression in courage was not the result of a calm consensus of all believing humankind, but from within the depth of the individual soul the lonely and anguished reliance on God alone. And such a situation continued to prevail in the subsequent ages as well. Luther noted that "St. Ambrose was alone in his day; after him, St. Jerome and St. Augustine. Furthermore, God did not choose many eminent and great bishops for this work. St. Augustine was bishop in one little unimportant city, but did he not accomplish more than all the Roman popes with all their fellow-bishops?"[17] What truly distinguished these saints and heroes was the capacity of their faith "to look away from self and to cling to the hand of God."[18] All the while these saints continued to remain sinners: "The weakness and struggle of the flesh with the spirit in the saints is ample testimony how weak their faith still is."[19] These saints did not win all their spiritual struggles; yet even in their very failures they learned to rely on God alone and to accept His help and blessing.[20] Without a doubt, Luther identified himself with such failing and winning saints. He saw the variants in their experience, and continued to appreciate the constant victory that occurred in weakness, through a lonely reliance on God in faith.

Without wishing to give an account of all such saints, we shall nevertheless mention a few of them. Here special attention, first of all, belongs to Noah, who in obedience to God began to build an ark on dry land: "This faith taught him to disdain the smugness of the world, which scoffed at him as at a deranged old man. This faith urged him to keep busy with the building of the ark, a structure which those notorious giants undoubtedly ridiculed as the utmost stupidity. This faith strengthened Noah to such an extent, that he stood alone in the face of so many examples of the world and courageously despised the opinions of all people."[21] Such faith—Noah's and, no doubt, also Luther's—was not a private heroic accomplishment, but a gift of the Holy Spirit.[22] The result was truly astounding: "To us today it seems impossible that one man should defy the entire world and condemn as evil all the rest...."[23] Having said this, and perhaps becoming aware how closely the portrait of Noah resembled his own visage, Luther hastened to observe the difference: "If I had been aware that so many men in the generation of the wicked were opposing me, I surely would have given up the ministry in despair. No one believes how difficult it is for one man to oppose the common opinion of all the churches, to contend against the views of very good men and very good friends, to condemn them, and to teach, live, and do everything in opposition to them. Noah did this because he was gifted with marvellous steadfastness. Blameless as he was before men, he not only did not leave God's business undone but carried it on courageously and with determination among the most wicked men...."[24] Whether or not there was such a difference between Noah and Luther is, of course, another matter. The fact remains that in retelling the story of Noah Luther did not mean to praise himself, but to point to the faithful example of others. It was in a similar vein that Luther referred to patriarch Abraham: "What should the patriarch Abraham have done when he had to move out of Chaldea (Gen. 12:1 ff.) and travel alone, as if he were the only Christian and the whole world were damned? But he could not let this divert him, nor could he pay attention to other people. Instead he had to say: 'How God deals with the whole world I will leave in His care. I will cling to His Word and follow that, regardless of whether I see the whole world going differently.'"[25]

While, by comparison, Isaac's life did not show great heroic deeds, Luther noted even there that the subsequent gift of the Holy Spirit suppled Isaac with courage.[26] So also Jacob was not only consoled but also encouraged by "the voice of God" whereupon remarkable deeds immediately followed: "After accepting the consolation, he musters up courage and dares what he would never have dared otherwise. Without the knowledge of his father-in-law and his sons, he dares to leave the house with his wife and his children and with all his possessions in full confidence."[27] Of all the patriarchs, however, Luther's favorite was Joseph, who "bore exile and imprisonment with unbroken courage."[28] It was the lengthy imprisonment in particular the elicited Luther's unqualified admiration—when "from hour to hour he expected punishment in prison and in hell." Yet, noted Luther, "he overcame these many tribulations with great courage. But to laugh at death and hell and to conquer is not the mark of a weakling; it is the mark of courage that is invincible, undaunted, and characteristic of a lion."[29]

All the while, Luther is clearly not referring to this exceptional kind of courage as a natural capacity of some people. Courage is gained through faith and again lost when faith itself crumbles. Such obtaining of faith, for example, Luther recognized ever so clearly in the faith-filled leadership activities of Moses: "...when they had already reached the boundaries of the Land of Promise, Moses sharpens their courage and arouses their faith by repeating the promise, so that they may enter without fear." But the true promises of God are never transmitted automatically and retained easily. Hence it happened with the followers of Moses as it often happens with adherents: "Here, however, faith wavers, and unbelief overwhelms the people in a pitiful demonstration, so that by their own fault, when they were ready at the point of entering the land to be occupied, they were forced to turn back and to wander thirty-eight years in the desert until they all perished...." Of this entire company only two men, Joshua and Caleb, had remained faithful and therefore they alone were permitted to enter the promised land. The others had been undone by unbelief which had started, as unbelief always starts, in an almost innocent-looking way: "This disaster of unbelief began with a small and innocent-looking doubt, when they pretended that they had to send spies who would show the way...." Beneath this pretense there lurked sin; they did not "believe the Word of God, who had given His promise, and had led them through the Red Sea where a way was impossible."[30] Courage and cowardice are therefore the immediate result of faith and unbelief, originating in response to God's Word of promise. Hence, whenever there are present any great accomplishments of courage, they must be recognized as the direct results of faith: "For by faith David struck down Goliath and gained all his victories. But whenever...[the Israelites] fought without faith and with only the power of numbers and troops, they were defeated."[31] For this reason the presence of faith suffices to anticipate the reality of subsequent courage. Observed Luther: "This is the quality of faith you see here on the part of the prophet David. He speaks with certainty and power about something that had not yet appeared or assumed reality."[32]

As must be noted, such true faith is always the result of "God's power and grace"—as may be recognized in the miraculous preservation and the ultimate success of prophet Jonah.[33] Here, as elsewhere, the final result of this courage of faith is not a mere record of human accomplishment, but an effective display of God's mighty saving acts. Luther remained observant: "But notice what an important office God entrusts to Jonah when He orders this one man to preach against the mighty empire of Assyria, against the king and his princes. After all, great lords dislike and resent being chided and being taken to task; they do not want to be rebuked. And now God commands Jonah here to upbraid them for their wickedness. That surely calls for genuine courage. Jonah has to open his mouth and speak."[34]

Realistically and autobiographically, Luther did not underestimate the power of courageous speaking. Far more important, however, was the witness of the scriptural precedent: "On Pentecost Peter stands up in Jerusalem, fears neither Annas or Caiphas nor the whole Sanhedrin, opens his mouth, strikes at the devil's kingdom, and with one sermon converts three thousand souls from the devil's kingdom to Christ. The other Apostles likewise turn on such power with their mouth and word that by it the synagog and the Jewish kingdom are run into the ground. Then they come to Rome, attack the highest power on earth, rebuke its paganism and idolatry, and with their mouths erect a power that no one can resist. They disperse further into the world, with the Word they storm the devil's kingdom, they plant and build Christ's church. Thus there comes the power which neither emperor nor king, neither princes nor potentates can resist. They oppose and fearfully abuse the Apostles and Christians, but to no avail. The power from the mouths of babes and sucklings slashes through and obtains the victory. Emperors, kings, and the potentates of the earth must hang their heads and confess that they cannot defend themselves against it."[35] In describing the courage of faith in the ancient past, was not Luther charting a similar course for the present as well? Certainly Luther envisioned that wherever true faith was to be proclaimed with courage, genuine conversions would not fail to follow. In saying this Luther did not attempt to forecast a membership in the millions, but only to witness that at the root of every great and popular faith-movement there lies a single, lonely person, wrestling with temptation and despair, who in the end nevertheless receives grace to believe and to live with courage. On one occasion Luther reflected as follows: "How the dear Virgin Mary must have felt when the angel came and brought her the message that she was to be the mother of the Highest (Luke 1:26ff.)! Who was standing near her and believed this or that supported her? Should she have considered the fact that there were available the daughters of so many rich, noble, and great lords and princes? Could not God have found any other one for this high work? Yet the only virgin He called to it was she, a poor, unknown, and despised maiden."[36] Although for the blessed Virgin Mary her faith bore visible results, Luther did not mean to suggest that courage must always consummate in success. Luther knew better: "Whenever I think of those saintly[37] men, John Hus[38] and Jerome of Prague, I reflect with the greatest admiration on their great courage; for these two men withstood the verdicts of the entire world—the pope, the emperor, the bishops, the princes, all the universities and schools throughout the empire."[39] Indeed, they withstood—but nevertheless perished in the flames at the Council of Constance in 1415. Luther had often thought about this fact: "St. John Hus—we can certainly do him the honor of calling him a saint, since he had far less guilt than we have—was burned at the stake of Constance. I have wondered very often how he, when he was all alone, could stand so firmly against the whole world, the pope, the emperor, and the entire council with not a single person to support him. On the contrary, he was condemned and cursed by everybody. Do you not suppose that for him prison often became narrow beyond endurance? Yet he had to comfort himself and overcome his fear with the very same verse with which Christ consoles himself: 'I am alone; yet I am not alone, for the Father is with Me.'"[40]

III.

Without a question, the Christian faith generates immense trust.[41] We call God "our Father"[42] and confess: "The great thing in life is to have a sure confidence in God...."[43] Yet having such a faith does not mean to possess this faith as one's personal property. As already noted, faith was gained in the very midst of life's struggles, when one was left without any other support than God alone. It is also in such a setting that faith is retained! Vividly, at times

Luther compared faith with a leap.[44] He wrote: "... we must leap from the safe shore of life into this abyss without seeing or feeling a sure footing under us. We must leap, as it were, at random, merely trusting to God's supporting and saving hand."[45] Here Luther was not imagining some relatively easy leap, as "across a moat or a brook" because for that kind of a leap "one who has neither strength nor agility employs skill and supports himself with a staff."[46] In the midst of life's real dangers there are no readily available supports, and therefore the believer must be ready for the kind of ultimate leap that Jonah had to make: "... thrown out of the ship ... [Jonah] plunges into the sea, feels no bottom, is deserted by all creatures and looks solely to God's sustaining power."[47] Or Luther could point to the universal inevitability of death, and then counsel the believer: "We must take a most perilous leap. My reason would judge that it is indeed a wretched life, to be carried out through the city gate, to be buried under the earth, and to be reduced to dust. And yet Christ declares that this is the way to gain life and to come to the Father. Therefore in that hour you must ignore physical death, the grave, pestilence, the sword, and the fire which you feel, also all the darts and spears the devil hurls into your heart. Instead, Christ says, 'You must look upon Me ... '"[48]

Because courage is not a cheap commodity, the risk[49] of faith cannot come easily! This is why our Lord warned Peter, in Luther's interpretation: "Look Peter, if you should preach my word and thus tend my sheep, then hell, the devil, the world, and everything in the world will rise against you. You will have to risk body, life, possessions, honor, friends, and everything you have. You will not do this unless you love me and steadfastly cling to me."[50] Luther did not doubt that such an authentic reliance was possible, and therefore challenged true preachers to risk all,[51] as well as on occasion admired the remarkable accomplishment of Frederick the Wise: "...our beloved elector openly confessed Christ's death and resurrection before the whole world and he stuck to it, staking his land and people, indeed his own body and life, upon it."[52]

In the final analysis, however, Luther always regarded the courage of faith to be a gift from God: "...the Holy Spirit must be present within us as the Paraclete, who encourages the heart so that we overcome joyfully, allow God to use our ministry; and are not at all frightened by the fear of death or sin..."[53] And, freely paraphrasing, Luther ascribed to Christ the following unjunction: "You must walk a path you do not know. How will you do that? Follow Me. I will fix My eyes on you. Just close your eyes and follow Me."[54] Elsewhere Luther summarized: "Therefore only that courage conquers which the Lord gives those whom He wants as victors."[55]

A further understanding of courage emerges, if with Luther we look at the location of courage within the human self.[56] Namely, Luther noted the difference between faith and hope, and located faith "in the intellect and hope in the will." Consequently, noted Luther, "faith commands and directs the intellect, though not apart from the will, and teaches what must be believed." At the same time it is hope that exhorts the will "because it arouses the mind to be brave and resolute, so that it dares, endures, and lasts in the midst of evils and looks for better things." Thus Luther compared hope to "a captain, battling against feelings such as tribulation, the cross, impatience, sadness, faintheartedness, despair, and blasphemy; and it battles with joy and courage, etc., in opposition to these great evils."[57]

While the analysis, offered with concepts of biblical theology, is clear, Luther sought to complement it with ideas borrowed from Classical thought. Namely, it is particularly in "the political realm" where we see that prudence and fortitude are related very closely, almost indistinguishably. Luther explained: "Now fortitude is a steadiness of mind, which does not despair in the midst of adversity but endures bravely and looks for better things. But unless fortitude is directed by prudence, it becomes rashness; on the other hand, unless fortitude is added to prudence, prudence is useless." Obviously, the explanation is not original, but is borrowed from Aristotle's *Nicomachean Ethics*.[58] In the end, Luther attempted to integrate biblical and Classical views and wrote: "Therefore just as in the political realm prudence is vain without fortitude, so in theology faith is nothing without hope, because hope endures and lasts in the midst of evils and conquers them. And, on the other hand, just as fortitude without prudence is rashness, so hope without faith is presumptuousness about the Spirit and a tempting of God; for since it lacks the knowledge of the truth or of Christ, which faith teaches it is a blind and rash fortitude.''[59]

Most consistently, however, Luther did not seek to offer further exposition of the dynamics of courage within the human self, but looked for the origins of courage in faith, and thereby meditated on God Himself. All the while Luther described courage in superlative terms; in other words, the courage about which Luther was concerned was never minor or mild, but God-inspired and therefore ultimate. Typically, Luther wrote: ''...faith...produces a daring and courage which enables one to hold anything on earth in contempt, to fear nothing at all, but in gay defiance to depend only on Christ, who rules eternally...''[60] And such a courage[61] was needed not only in regard to earthly opponents but even *vis-a-vis* God Himself, notably when the believer was confronted by the hidden God: ''What, then, are human powers, where faith and the Word reign, except masks of God,[62] as it were, under which He hides and does His wonders, while through their weakness He stirs up the proud, brave, wise, and holy against Himself?''[63] Luther's main point was that the believer, in faith and with courage, was able to see through these masks: ''Faith does not despair of the God who sends trouble. Faith does not consider Him angry or an enemy, as the flesh, the world, and the devil strongly suggest. Faith rises above all this and sees God's fatherly heart behind His unfriendly exterior. Faith sees the sun shining through these thick, dark clouds and this gloomy weather. Faith has the courage to call with confidence to Him who smites it and looks at it with such a sour face.''[64] Such a faith, Luther was convinced, had to be a gift from God: ''The flesh cannot by itself believe in God. It cannot but fear the world and its enemies. We have, therefore, a need for the Spirit as our Strengthener and Encourager. When He comes, He so encourages us that we shun nothing for the sake of the glory of God, we dare all things. We even draw near to God.''[65]

Without denying the possibility of a miraculous intervention by God, Luther ordinarily viewed the Holy Spirit as reaching the believers through the instrumentality of the Word. E.g.: ''But when the heart takes hold of the Word, then the enlightenment of the Holy Spirit follows, and the power and might to do amazing things."[66] "...a right faith goes right on with its eyes closed; it clings to God's Word; it follows that Word; it believes the Word even when all creatures are against, even if it should seem to the flesh that nothing is less likely to happen than what the Word wants and to happen, even if heaven and earth should first seem to be destined to pass away."[67] Therefore courage, which had been generated in this manner, could not be suppressed—since the work of God is indestructible. Luther explained in regard to his situation: "The pope had no shortage of learned, wise, and intelligent people, and is far ahead of us in skill, brains, and intelligence. Yet he does not get anywhere against us. We do nothing but open our mouths and speak the Word boldly. We wage a battle with the pope in which we wield no sword and shoot no guns. Yet with the Word, the Our Father, the children's Creed, and the Gospel we erect a power which is so strong and mighty that it mows down the system of priests, monks, and nuns as well as the whole papacy."[68] Therefore, Luther exhorted: "Let no one be scared by their damnation, persecution, and madness. Here we have the assurance that those who teach God's Word purely and truly and cling to it shall be great before Christ in the kingdom of heaven in spite of the fact that this mob may curse them to the lowest hell."[69]

IV.

While emphasizing the exclusively Christian context for the emergence of authentic courage, Luther at times also made use of the classical roots of the concept of courage.[70] Familiar with Roman literature, Luther marvelled at the heights to which Roman courage had risen. Some of these observations were purely factual without any further attempt at theological explanation. On one such occasion Luther related: "Midwives should be full of courage, and, as Vergil says in Aeneas, feign hope in their countenance,[71] console a woman laboring in chilbirth, and bid her be of good hope. For in a wonderful way hope buoys up the spirits of those who are weighed down by misfortunes and sufferings, as Aeneas adds: 'God will grant an end also to these.'[72] Such prudence and courage is also required in a midwife, in order that when the danger is present and manifest, she may have great hope in her heart and

115

with her words may also kindle the same hope in the woman in labor.''[73] Similarly non-theological is another brief reference to the fact of courage in classical antiquity: ''Vergil relates about Aeneas that he encouraged his comrades by the examples of former liberations. Aeneas says: 'O comrades—for we are not without knowledge of former woes—O you who have suffered heavier woes, the god will put an end to these too!'[74] He also says that every misfortune must be overcome by bearing it. We must never stop or leave off.[75] But if the heathen overcame difficulties of every kind with such stout courage, why should we allow this courage to be missing in us Christians?''[76] Clearly, this is not merely a question, but a serious exhortation. Of such Luther employs several. His favorite text comes from Vergil: ''Therefore this is an exhortation to us not to despair, but to keep our courage unbroken in order to bear these evils to the end. It is as though he were saying: 'Suffer and bear. Do noy yield to evils, but rather go forth even more boldly!'''[77] How closely Luther has at times mingled classical and Christian motifs may be noted from his use of the above exhortation together with a quotation from the New Testament and an autobiographical reference: ''Therefore rouse yourself. Do not give in to evils, but go forth more boldly against them.[78] Hold on, do not be disheartened either by contempt or ingratitude within or by agitation or raging without. But think as follows: 'When I am weak, I am strongest' (2 Cor. 12:10); when I am suppressed, I rise up, as a palm rises up under its burden. So they thought that we had perished at Augsburg, but there we rose highest of all. Similarly it is in sorrow, when we are the closest to despair, that hope rises the highest.''[79]

Most often, however, in using classical sources, Luther pointed to God as the author of the truths which they contain. Luther wrote: ''Truth comes from the Holy Spirit, regardless of who says it, especially the true sayings of the poets, when they show us our sins.''[80] Occasionally Luther employed a typological exegesis, and applied it to the classical sources as he had done it to the Old Testament. The results could be remarkable: ''...this promise of the Holy Spirit has been adumbrated in this text by means of the analogy of drunkennes from an excellent vine. For as a drunken man is bolder and more courages—the poet says: 'Then a poor man musters up courage,[81] to such an extent that one man has the audacity to oppose himself to a hundred others—so that spiritual, holy, and salutary drunkenness adds much more courage to the godly who swell with divine power..."[82] At other times Luther interpreted the classical concept of "fortuna" as a gift from God: "In war, fortune rules. It is a large-scale affair that cannot be ruled by human prudence, for nowhere does fortune respond to counsel less than in war. Therefore good fortune must be divinely given, and angels must be present with the man who conquers."[83] At the same time Luther assumed that the "heathen" were ignorant of the divine source of fortune: "The heathen could not know the source of such a difference among princes. They called it 'fortune' or 'luck' and made a goddess out of it. They honored her very highly, especially the wisest and most powerful lords at Rome. The very wisest among them, like Cicero, say it is a divine inspiration; and they conclude that no one has ever become a great man through his own powers but only by a special secret inbreathing or imparting of the gods."[84] In a Christian perspective, Luther connected fortune with a direct intervention by God. And without suggesting that he could discern the purpose of such divine protection, he nevertheless proposed the following basic rationale: "Because God willed to give temporal dominion to the heathen or to reason, He also had to provide people who had wisdom and courage, who had the necessary inclination and skill, and who would preserve it."[85]

Proceeding in this manner, Luther succeeded in integrating the classical references within his basic theological framework. The significance of such an achievement for Luther's theology was not minor, as it allowed Luther to assign to courage a consistently derivative and dependent status. Courage was possible only on account of faith which in turn was a gift of God! In this way while celebrating courage, Luther successfully avoided the pitfall of praising himself for having had the courage to set a reformation in progress.

Yet while guarding against the sin of pride in one regard, Luther did not build his defenses with sufficient thoroughness. According to Luther, courage, and the faith from which courage flowed, was essentially an individualistic accomplishment, as ultimate courage was reached not in a consensus situation but in complete loneliness.[86] Most often Luther suggested no higher standard that could measure the correctness of his own courageous faith. With pathos, convinced of his own total theological righteousness, Martin Luther proclaimed: "Therefore my doctrine is true, pure, sure, and divine. Nor can there be any doctrine that is different from mine, much less better."[87] And precisely because Luther was convinced of his absolute theological—not necessarily moral—rightness, he felt justified to reject all those who differed from him: "With Paul, therefore, we boldly and confidentially pronounce a curse upon any doctrine that does not agree with ours."[88] "With Paul we boast that we teach the pure Gospel of Christ."[89] Of course, Luther was not unaware that his stance could be and was questioned. But instead of a self-defense, Luther offered a spirited attack: "I know that the pious should be humble; but in opposition to the pope I am willing and obliged to be proud with a holy pride and to say: 'I refuse to be subject to you, pope. I refuse to accept you as my master, for I am certain that my doctrine is true and godly. And I can prove it with sound arguments!' … Accursed be any humility that yields or submits at this point! Rather let everyone be proud and unremitting here, unless he wants to deny Christ. With the help of God, therefore, I will be more hardheaded than anyone else. I want to be stubborn and to be known as someone who is stubborn. Here I bear the inscription 'I yield to no one.'"[90]

Fortunately, Luther did not always write with such an uncompromising and self-righteous fervor. He then built his theology on the clear and convincing exegesis of the Word of God, and challenged those who did not follow the Scriptures[91]—but at the same time showed immense political realism in dealing with the power structures of his day.[92] Nevertheless, Luther's courage of faith, ready to inspire and to lead to Jesus Christ, also continued to sustain the pleasant but mistaken persuasion, that the complete truth had been already reached either by exegesis or by reason redeemed by grace.[93] Thus the courage of faith which, rightly, drove Luther to assert that "the Holy Spirit is not a skeptic!"[94] also lead Luther, quite unfortunately, to regard his own faith as the only true one, and his courage as the ultimate act of loyalty to God.

To state this, however, is not to wish that Luther would have been another man than he actually was. To wait for the emergence of perfect saints that would renew the church in a perfect manner would leave the church unreformed. Luther did what he believed to be a Christian duty in his own day, and we must have the courage to celebrate his courage and God's grace in our own day.

ENDNOTES

The author's gratitude is expressed to the Faculty Fellowship Division of the Social Sciences and Humanities Research Council of Canada which has enabled the research for this study.

1. Heiko A. Oberman sums up: "Als die Kirche dem Himmel noch gleich war und der Kaiser die Macht der Welt repraesentierte, da hatte sich dieser Moench gegen die Maechte von Himmel und Erde erhoben," *Luther: Mensch zwischen Gott und Teufel* (Berlin: Severin und Siedler, 1981), p. 7.

2. WA 31,I:112:1-2; LW 14:67.

3. WA 32:346:14-16; LW 21:57.

4. WA 7:838:9; LW 32:113. "Ich kan nicht anderst, hie stehe ich, Gott helf mir, Amen." In the actual record of the diet the text reads crisply: "Gott helf mir. Amen." (May God help me. Amen.) *Deutsche Reichstagsakten, Juengere Reihe: Deutsche Reichstagsakten unter Kaiser Karl V.*, Gotha, 1896, II:587. The 1546 Wittenberg edition includes the more powerful text, *Reichstagsakten*, II:555.37. Cf. Oberman, p. 47, who notes the often overlooked fact that the nation heard the longer and the more impressive version! The fact remains that the shorter version is regarded as the authentic one, e.g. Hellmut Diwald, *Luther: Eine Biographie* (Bergisch Gladbach: Gustav Luebbke, 1982), p. 196; Horst Herrmann, *Martin Luther: Ketzer wider Willen* (Muenchen: C. Bertelsmann, 1983) p. 254; Walther von Loewenich, *Martin Luther: Der Mann und das Werk* (Muenchen: List, 1982), p. 185.

5. WA 15:214:24-26; LW 40:53. Even though printed only in 1529, Luther's *A Mighty Fortress* expresses his faith and courage, especially in verse 3, and may have been written during the journey to Worms, cf. Diwald, pp. 189-190.

6. Certainly this had not been the first occasion which had caused Luther to be worried. The encounter with Cardinal Cajetan in Augsburg, 1518, had also been a traumatic event, cf. Martin Brecht, *Martin Luther: Sein Weg zur Reformation 1483-1521* (Stuttgart: Calwer Verlag, 1981), p. 248.

7. WA 12:239:18; LW 45:151.

8. WA 8:482:32-483:1-4; LW 35:134. The concern had been his already at an earlier date as well: "True, when I was a young master at Erfurt, I was often downcast due to assaults of gloominess. Thus I devoted myself mostly to reading the Bible. In this way, from the naked text of the Bible, I soon recognized many errors in the papacy. But there in the library at Erfurt many thoughts came upon me such as: 'Behold, how great is the authority of the pope and the church! Are you alone supposed to be clever? Oh, you might be mistaken!' I yielded to these thoughts and suffered quite a setback in reading the Bible!" WA TR 3:437:2-8, nr. 3593, 1537, quoted by Scott H. Hendrix, *Luther and the Papacy: Stages in a Reformation Conflict* (Philadelphia: Fortress, 1981), p. 6. Luther's positive response to doubt was best formulated in his *Explanations of the Ninety-five Theses*, 1518, where he declared: "I am not the only one: the truth is on my side," WA 1:611:10; LW 31:221. Cf. Emanuel Hirsch, "Luthers Beziehung auf das Gewissen in seinem Kampf

mit der Papstkirche," I:172-220, in *Lutherstudien* (Guetersloh: C. Bertelsmann, 1954).

9. WA 31,I:101:27-30; LW 14:63.

10. Harmannus Obendiek speaks of "the dynamic character of the Word" and suggests that where there is no tribulation, there is also no presence of the Word. At the same time, when present, the Word does not act in a magical manner, but requires an authentic human response in courageous faith. *Der Teufel bei Martin Luther* (Berlin: Furche Verlag, 1931), pp. 159-165.

11. WA 31, II:284:31-35; LW 17:31. Cf. Horst Beintker, *Die Ueberwindung der Anfechtung bei Luther* (Berlin: Evangelische Verlagsanstalt, 1954); Erwin Muelhaupt, "Luthers Kampf mit der Krankheit," *Luther: Zeitschrift der Luther Gesellschaft*, 29(1958):115-123; Peter Meinhold, "Zur Theologie der Krankheit bei Martin Luther," *Saeculum*, 23(1972):15-29; Ulrich Becke, "Eine hinterlassene psychiatrische Studie Paul Johann Reiters ueber Luther," *Zeitschrift fuer Kirchengeschichte*, 90(1979):85-95; Walther von Loewenich, pp. 358-364.

12. WA 31,II:397:2-4; LW 17:173-174. Cf. Bernhard Lohse, *Ratio und Fides: Eine Untersuchung ueber die ratio in der Theologie Luthers* (Goettingen: Vandenhoeck & Ruprecht, 1958), p. 49; B.A. Gerrish, *Grace and Reason: A Study in the Theology of Luther* (Oxford: At the Clarendon Press, 1962), pp. 10-27; Karl-Heinz zur Muehlen, *Reformatorische Vernunftkritik und neuzeitliches Denken: Dargestellt am Werk M. Luthers und Fr. Gogartens* (Tuebingen: J.C.B. Mohr [Paul Siebeck], 1980).

13. "I, Martin Luther, cannot teach the faith without experiencing this conflict daily. Faith is based solely on trust in God and on the grace of God." WA 31,II:426:22-24; LW 17:213.

14. WA 31,II:459:5-7; LW 17:256.

15. WA 33:114b:12-25; LW 23:76.

16. WA 7:311:23-29; LW 32:8.

17. WA 7:313:7-12; LW 32:9.

18. WA 31,I:149:28-30; LW 14:85.

19. WA 40,I:599:16-18; LW 26:393.

20. "Because when a godly person is aware of his fall, he becomes ashamed and is perturbed. Thus his fall leads first to humility and then also to fervent prayer." WA 43:115:9-11; LW 3:334. "But God is wonderful in His saints, and so wonderful that through their failings and errors He manifests His wisdom to us." WA 43:145:21-22; LW 4:14.

21. WA 42:281:22-26; LW 2:28.

22. "Hence we draw the universal conclusion that without the Holy Spirit and without grace man can do nothing but sin and so goes on endlessly from sin to sin." WA 42:290:14-16; LW 2:40.

23. WA 42:301:15-17; LW 2:56.

24. WA 42:301:30-36; LW 2:56.

25. WA 32:501:23-28; LW 21:243-244. Cf. WA 42:462:35-39, 463:1-16; LW 2:281-282.

26. WA 43:522:7-8; LW 5:136.

27. WA 44:7:9-12; LW 6:11.

28. WA 44:425:23-24; LW 7:170.

29. WA 44:427:19-22; LW 7:172-173.

30. WA 14:555:24-31; LW 9:20.

31. WA 691:30-32; LW 9:202.

32. WA 41:97:17-19; LW 13:242.

33. WA 19:186:16; LW 19:36.

34. WA 19:195:13-18; LW 19:42.

35. WA 45:221:25-38, 222:10-11; LW 12:111.

36. WA 32:501:17-23; LW 21:243.

37. Cf. Lennart Pinomaa, *Die Heiligen bei Luther* (Helsinki, 1977), p. 61.

38. History is often filled with irony. When in 1505 as a novice Luther was received into the Augustinian monastery at Erfurt, he had, according to custom, prostrated himself upon the ground—which happened to be the place of burial of Johannes Zacharia, who in 1415 at Constance had debated against John Hus. For this accomplishment the pope awarded him the golden rose which Zacharia, the *Hussomastix* (the overcomer of Hus), henceforth proudly wore on his doctoral beret! Hellmut Diwald, p. 106. For Luther's views of Hus, cf. Jaroslav Pelikan, *Obedient Rebels: Catholic Substance and Protestant Principle in Luther's Reformation* (New York: Harper & Row, 1964), pp. 110-119, 136-146.

39. WA 42:324:17-20; LW 2:87-88. Cf. WA 44:774:19-25; LW 8:266.

40. WA 46:103:12-20; LW 24:413.

41. WA 14:633:2-7; LW 9:96.

42. WA 2:83:10-86:13; LW 42:23.

43. WA 6:208:10-12; LW 44:28.

44. Søren Kierkegaard continued to interpret the meaning of faith and often relied on the

metaphor of a "leap," most vividly in *Fear and Trembling and The Sickness unto Death* (New York: Doubleday Anchor Books, 1954), pp. 51-52; and in *The Concept of Anxiety* (Princeton University Press, 1980), pp. 131-132; cf. also the *Concluding Unscientific Postscript* (Princeton University Press, 1944), pp. 15, 90-97, 105, 231, 262, 306, 327, 340, 343.

45. WA 19:217:20-22; LW 19:66.

46. WA 43:63:1-5; LW 3:262.

47. WA 19:217:23-25; LW 19:66.

48. WA 45:505:35-38, 506:1-4; LW 24:49-50.

49. For a very brief, but insightful statement, cf. Robert H. Fischer, "The Risk of Luther's Reformation," *Dialog* (1976):176-183.

50. WA 6:320:8-12; LW 39:99.

51. "When a peasant becomes greedy and contributes nothing to the support of the Gospel, a preacher can still be provided for, if only very meagerly. But when the preachers themselves succumb to it, they lose their taste for the Gospel. They are not willing to suffer anything or risk anything for its sake. They try to figure out how to keep their belly well supplied, and they will preach whatever is pleasing to their audience and financially profitable to them." WA 32:454:27-38; LW 21:177.

52. WA 36:246:14-17; LW 51:237.

53. WA 13:578:8-10; LW 20:36, cf. 40,II:554:27-33; LW 12:258-259, and WA 45:568:35, 569:1; LW 24:118.

54. WA 31,II:321:4-6; LW 17:76.

55. WA 13:586:27, 587:1; LW 20:44.

56. For on overview of Luther's definition of the self, cf. Herbert Olsson, *Schoepfung, Vernunft und Gesetz in Luthers Theologie* (Uppsala, 1971), pp. 454-570, and Bengt Haeglund, "Luthers Anthropologie," pp. 62-76, in Helmar Junghans, ed., *Leben und Werk Martin Luthers von 1526 bis 1546* (Berlin: Evangelisch Verlagsanstalt, 1983).

57. WA 40,II:26:11-21; LW 27:22.

58. III,6-9.

59. WA 40,II:27:23-32; LW 27:23.

60. WA 41:98:14-16; LW 13:243.

61. Paul Hacker has critically noted that Luther has incorporated in his perspective a sense of "obstinate defiance" (Trotz), combining with "consolation" (Trost), *The Ego in Faith:*

Martin Luther and the Origin of Anthropocentric Religion (Chicago: Franciscan Herald Press, 1970), p. 128.

62. Cf. Hanns Lilje, *Luthers Geschichtsauffassung* (Berlin: Furche, 1932), pp. 68-123; Heinrich Bornkamm, "Der verborgene und der offenbare Gott," pp. 68-88, in *Luthers geistige Welt* (Guetersloh: C. Bertelsmann, 1953), English trans. *Luther's World of Thought* (St. Louis: Concordia Publishing House, 1958), pp. 55-74; John Dillenberger, *God Hidden and Revealed* (Philadelphia: Muhlenberg Press, 1953); Hellmut Bandt, *Luthers Lehre vom verborgenen Gott: Eine Untersuchung zu dem offenbarungsgeschichtlichen Ansatz seiner Theologie* (Berlin: Evangelische Verlagsanstalt, 1958); David Loefgren, *Die Theologie der Schoepfung bei Luther*) Goettingen: Vandenhoeck & Ruprecht, 1960), pp. 225-240; Hans-Martin Barth, *Der Teufel und Jesus Christus in der Theologie Martin Luthers* (Goettingen: Vandenhoeck &Ruprecht, 1967), pp. 185-188; Rudolf Herrman, *Luthers Theologie,* ed. Horst Beintker (Goettingen: Vandenhoeck & Ruprecht, 1967), pp. 158-164; Reinhold Weier, *Das Thema von verborgenen Got von Nikolaus Kues zu Martin Luther* (Muenster, Westf.: Verlag Aschendorff, 1967); Beinhold Weier, *Das Theologieverstaendnis Martin Luthers* (Paderborn: Verlag Bonifacius Druckerei, 1967); B.A. Gerrish, "To An Unknown God: Luther and Calvin on the Hiddenness of God," *Journal of Religion,* 53(1973):263-292; Tarald Rasmussen, "Posteriora Dei: Ein biblischer Begriff des Redens Luthers von Gottes Verborgenheit," *Kerygma und Dogma,* 25(1979):209-230.

63. WA 14:577:34-37; LW 9:41; cf. WA 40,II:54:15-16; LW 27:43.

64. WA 31,I:93:16-17, 94:1-5; LW 14:59.

65. WA 13:539:7-10; LW 18:387. Luther precedes this by explaining: "*The Spirit.* This is enthusiasm, *Mut.* The Germans use this word in various ways. *Er hat einen Mut;* that is, he is proud; he is also full of life. He is endowed with a certain strength of mind to endure adverse situations bravely. This God the Spirit stirs up in us when God breathes upon us with His Spirit, when he causes in us through the Spirit the courage and confidence to finish something we have begun and to which we otherwise would scarcely aspire in our timidity. To be sure, the Holy Spirit is like that because we tremble in God's business." WA 13:539:1-7; LW 18:378.

66. WA 43:520:8-9; LW 5:133. As a rule, Luther did not give any credit to nature, but attributed all courage to the working of grace. Luther scholars have, however, at times noted Luther's "natural assertiveness," cf. Scott H. Hendrix, op. cit., p. 27.

67. WA 13:244:16-19; LW 19:8.

68. WA 45:224:32-39; LW 12:114.

69. WA 32:359:9-12; LW 21:72, cf. WA 32:503:8-10; LW 21:246.

70. Luther was not guilty of what Jaroslav Pelikan has so aptly called "the blasphemous separation between the realm of nature and the realm of grace," "Luther Comes to the New World," p. 4, in Heiko A. Oberman, ed., *Luther and the Dawn of the Modern Era: Papers of the Fourth International Congress for Luther Research* (Leiden: E.J. Brill, 1974). At the same time, of course, Luther ordinarily accented the work of grace.

71. *Aeneid*, I,209.

72. Ibid., I,199.

73. WA 44:336:34-40; LW 7:48.

74. *Aeneid*, I,198-199.

75. Ibid., V, 710.

76. WA 44:449:36-41; LW 7:203.

77. *Aeneid*, VI, 95.

78. Ibid., VI, 95.

79. WA 40,II:502:27-32; LW 12:220.

80. WA 25:33:1-3; LW 29:38. Ordinarily Luther regarded the insights of unbelievers, when valid, to have been attained by their natural reason, cf. Harry J. McSorley, *Luther: Right or Wrong? An Ecumenical-Theological Study of Luther's Major Work* The Bondage of the Will (New York: Newman Press, and Minneapolis: Augsburg Publishing House, 1969), p. 311.

81. Ovid, *Ars amandi*, I, 239.

82. WA 44:764:11-16; LW 8:252.

83. WA 40:511:16-19; LW 12:226.

84. WA 51:244:21-27; LW 13:200-201. Philip S. Watson, *Let God Be God: An Interpretation of the Theology of Martin Luther* (Philadelphia: Muhlenberg Press, 1950), p. 93 notes that "Cicero and men like him may be saved," referring to WA TR 372, nr. 626. Ordinarily Luther scholarship has tended to emphasize the uniquely saving role of Jesus Christ, e.g., Walter Holsten, *Christentum und nichtchristliche Religion nach der Auffassung Luthers* (Guetersloh: C. Bertelsmann, 1932); Ernst Wolf, "Das Evangelium und die Religion," pp. 9-29 in *Peregrinatio: Studien zur reformatorischen Theologie und zum Kirchenproblem* (Muenchen: Chr. Kaiser, 1954); Egil Grislis, "Luther and the Turks," *The Muslim World*, 64,3(1974):180-193 and 64,4(1974):275-291.

85. WA 51:243:13-16; LW 13:199.

86. That the necessary reliance on the Word—see above, ftn. 8—is not a completely subjective undertaking, follows from Luther's understanding of the creative role of conscience, cf. Bernhard Lohse, "Conscience and Authority in Luther," pp. 158-183 in Heiko A. Oberman, *Luther and the Dawn of the Modern Era;* cf. Herbert Olsson, pp. 562-570.

87. WA 40,I:122:30-31; LW 26:59.

88. WA 40,I:123:15-17; LW 26:59. For a sympathetic account, cf. Hans-Werner Gensichen, *We Condemn: How Luther and 16th Century Lutheranism Condemned False Doctrine* (St. Louis: Concordia Publishing House, 1967), pp. 61-79. Unfortunately, at times Luther was prepared to use force against dissidents, e.g., John S. Oyer *Lutheran Reformers against Anabaptists: Luther, Melanchthon and Menius and the Anabaptists in Central Germany (The Hague: Martinus Nijhoff, 1964), pp. 118-119, 123-124.*

89. *WA 40,I:133:18-19; LW 26:67.*

90. *WA 40,I:180:19-22; LW 26:98-99. In 1509 Alexander Stuart of Scotland had given to his teacher Erasmus a signet ring with the image of the god Terminus and the inscription: "Concedo nulli," "I yield to no one." Just what Erasmus understood this expression to mean had been widely discussed. Cf. Ernest Wilhelm Kohls, Die Theologie des Erasmus* (Basel: Friedrich Reinhard Verlag, 1966)II:42-43; Roland H. Bainton, *Erasmus of Christendom* (New York: Charles Scribner's Sons, 1969), p. 87.

91. Cf. Dietrich Kerlen, *Assertio: Die Entwicklung von Luthers theologischem Anspruch und der Streit mit Erasmus von Rotterdam* (Wiesbaden: Franz Steiner, 1976), pp. 87-90.

92. Cf. Hermann Kunst, *Evangelischer Glaube und politische Verantwortung: Martin Luther als politischer Berater* (Stuttgart: Evangelisches Verlagswerk, 1976); Quentin Skinner, *The Foundations of Modern Political Thought.* Vol. II: *The Age of Reformation* (Cambridge University Press, 1978).

93. Bernhard Lohse, *Ratio und Fides,* p. 101.

94. WA 18:605:32; LW 33:24. Gordon Rupp catches Luther's mood perfectly: "The word 'scepticism' enraged Luther," *The Righteousness of God: Luther Studies* (London: Hodder and Stoughton, 1953), p. 272.